100 Leadership Nuggets

By Dr. David Robinson PhD

Dr. David Robinson

Other books and leadership material may be ordered
through booksellers or contacting:

City Limits International
PO Box 6086
Elgin, Illinois 60121
www.coaching4ministers.com
www.daverobinsoncoach.com

100 Days

100 Days

To Marie,

The light of my life and the love of my heart for the past 50 years!

Endorsements

When Dr. Dave Robinson speaks on Leadership....I listen! His biblical insight coupled with his practical wisdom and experience have inspired me to reach for greater effectiveness as a leader.

I am very happy to recommend his new book, "100 Leadership Nuggets." I promise you that these powerful daily truths will enrich your life and encourage you to become a greater person as well as a greater leader.

—Garry D. Smith
Pastor / CityGate Church

....

From the heart of a leader, you will receive power packed snippets of truth that will help propel you into your next season of greatness and sustain your current season of growth and leadership.

Whether in ministry or a marketplace career, this book will become a favorite "go to" for encouragement and inspiration.

—Pastor Tim Walker,
The Entrepreneur's Pastor

....

There are certain people that have such a significant impact on our lives by compelling us to not only thing big but gives great insight on how to think. David's leadership nuggets do exactly that! So challenging at times but such rewarding results! I have no doubt you will find this book (Leadership Nuggets) a major help on how to arrive at right answers for reoccurring challenges. I Did!

—Jeremy LaBorde, Senior Pastor/Founder Gloryland Church
Founder, Jeremy LaBorde Ministries International

....

David's Leadership Nuggets will be on my personal must-read list and I will share them with as many of my friends and colleagues as possible! David's 100 Leadership Nuggets are easy to read, straight to the point, at times they feel a bit too much 'in-your-face-kind', however knowing David's heart to equip and empower leaders, I will take his teaching on leadership over anyone else's.

My other option would be to not learn and glean from David's wisdom and become a personal and an organizational liability. As you read the nuggets, you will see how God has invested in David's life wisdom and discernment that he now shares without hesitation but with a little bit of holding back—he knows that we all are busy and probably have already read most everything that you can find in a bookstore or online—so, he's holding back really is more for the purpose of getting down the bottom line issues and questions. All 100 Nuggets will stir up your thinking (not only Day 64!), will make you ask some hard questions, and will help you solve the impossible (Day 95).

—Nasko D. Lazarov
Global Action, Colorado Springs, CO

I love the leadership insights and principles that Dave put in this newest book. Anyone can read them at any time and receive insight and golden keys to management and leadership. Dave shares these from many years of experience in both the pastorate and the marketplace. This is a great tool and will be one that you turn to from time to and be reminded and refreshed.

Even those of us who are already successful leaders will be enhanced and your thinking enlarged. Every one of us have been "stuck" from time to time and these keys are the tow truck that gets you moving again. A great reference tool. It would make a great gift to any leader or future leader. Great job Dave. Proud of you and your work.

—Dr. Mark T Barclay
Mark Barclay Ministries

Forward

David Robinson's work is quite literally incomparable. Whether it be his passion for his faith or the leadership work he does around the globe, he is undoubtedly wholehearted in his approach to any subject. David is a person whom once you are acquainted with him, you know exactly what you are going to get.

I met David about six years ago through a mutual relationship. As a professional Behavioral Analyst and Profiler, our unique meeting was designed around my behavioral analysis and the debrief that followed. In Dave's words; "When he told me he liked to jam a fork in people's neck's so he could drain out their nonsense, I knew I was going to like this guy."

Since then David has become an integral part of my life. In many ways, he's like a brother and in others a father. His no nonsense approach to leadership and integrity have been critical buoy's in the sea that surrounds me. His openness, reliability, and fatherly influence are attributes I will always cherish in David. His latest work, 100 Nuggets, is more than just a book.

It's a mineshaft. For those who are in need of practical wisdom and a sense of direction this work will be unmatched by many. It's a trip into David's heart. A no holds bar approach to effectiveness in life and work. My prayer for you is that you find yourself the time to mine through every subject in this book with an open heart and a clean slate.

Allow his life experiences to permeate your soul and influence your decisions for best practices. I love you David.

Thank you so much for your continued contribution to the world and the people in it.

—Steve Sisler
President and founder of The Behavioral Resource Group, Inc. and Sisler Solutions, LLC.

Introduction

"Change—Every Leader's Greatest Challenge"

Astronaut James Irwin said, "You might think going to the moon was the most scientific project ever, but they literally 'threw us' in the direction of the moon. We had to adjust our course every ten minutes and landed only fifty feet inside of a 500-mile radius of our target." On that mission, every change, no matter how small, was essential to success.

Resisting change and defending the status quo only proves that you have no intention of changing. Almost everyone favors progress and dreams of how things could or should be. Its change they do not like. Great leaders are not only willing to change, but change is a way of life for them. Good leaders change when they see the light and poor leaders only change when they feel the heat.

Wise leaders are willing to change their minds, their heart and even their behavior when change is uncomfortable. Willingness to change is a sign of strength-- not weakness. Fools seldom make changes even when it really matters. Stubborn fools do not hold opinions; their opinions hold them and the entire organization suffers.

Believing in change is not the same as embracing change by making significant behavioral changes from the front office to the front line. The mettle of any leadership team is leading change when it makes the most difference, not necessarily when it makes the most sense.

Change is a process, not an event. Change works when all team members stay energized, engaged and adequately informed throughout the process. Change seldom happens when managing leaders are in charge because their gifting and nature is maintaining the status quo. It takes strategic [apostolic] leaders who, by gifting, constantly declare war on the status quo.

Changes come in two forms

First, leaders make a declaration or send out an edict calling for change. If you have enough money, power, authority and time, you can effect change without team members' approval, energy or engagement. *"It's my way or the highway"* does not work anymore.

Second, team members make behavioral changes. This requires a lot of relational equity on the part of core leaders and buy-in by everyone. On average, it takes at least 70% of your front-line leaders supporting change once there is 100% consensus by core leaders. If you try implementing change without this kind of support, positive results seldom occur.

What causes a lack of behavioral change? People are seldom the problem but most often get the blame. Senior leaders create most of the problems preventing change by their lack of leadership in the following four areas:

1. Lack of clarity about the goals and strategy for change. People cannot buy in to what they cannot see or understand. This clarity diminishes in proportion to the distance a person moves away from the core leaders.
2. Lack of commitment and passion modeled by core leaders for the Mission, Vision, and Values of your

organization or ministry. It is difficult to stay focused and energized about anything that you have not committed to memory and then make the eighteen-inch transfer to your heart. You are only passionate about what you truly believe and find worthy of investing your time and energy.

3. Lack of accountability on a regular basis to reinforce positive sustainable results. Without accountability, there is no way to improve, much less change.
4. Lack of trust in the leadership's abilities and decision-making skills.

However, the **Number One Enemy** in making change, seizing new opportunities, and overcoming active inertia is the urgency to protect and maintain what you already have.

Whatever you focus on the most is what you produce the most. It does not matter if it is the past, present, or future. Whether it works or does not work. Whether it is relevant or irrelevant, your focus determines your outcomes, not how many meetings you conduct or how long and detailed your discussions.

Every team member has a responsible role in achieving the goal for making change happen. Everyone must know the following four things or change is difficult at best or never takes place at worst.

1. Everyone knows the goals for change and can state them clearly.
2. Everyone knows what it will take to achieve individual and team success.
3. Everyone knows the "score" at any time, as a team and their individual effort.

4. Everyone knows they are accountable individually, to their leader, and their team.

Leadership is all about change and creating the future, management is about bringing control to the chaos created by leaders in their pursuit of the future. I teach everyone is a leader by influence not so much by position or title. Whether you are a leader who clears the brush and creates the path forward, or a manger overseeing the daily tasks and leading the teams you will find help in these daily leadership thoughts.

I designed "100 Daily Leadership Nuggets" as a handbook for those beginning their leadership journey or an anchor for the seasoned leader experiencing some rough waters along the way. You can read them in five minutes and reflect throughout the day how you can implement the truths that best fit your leadership challenges.

Every leader and manager makes a difference, the question is what kind and how much?

Dr. David Robinson

Day 1
3 Reasons Why Team Members Disappoint You

Unfulfilled or misplaced expectations bring life's greatest disappointments regardless of the relationship. As a leader, one of your top priorities is defining and communicating performance expectations; if you do not, you can expect conflict, misunderstanding and high staff turnover for starters. I guarantee you the good and above average do not stick around long.

What are the three top reasons for unfilled expectations? Your team does not know what is expected—information, they do not know how—skill development, or they do not want to—motivation. Whatever the reason your task is helping them make the necessary adjustments and improvements. If your team is not fulfilling your expectations—look in the mirror that is where solving your problem begins. Most leaders create most of their own disappointments.

Job Descriptions do not solve unfulfilled expectations. The best job description in the world does not guarantee superior performance, good performance, or even adequate performance. At best, it gives a general overview of responsibilities and functional expectations, and sometimes it can be detrimental to performing well if not properly understood.

Three terms every leader needs to understand and use consistently

A Performance Agreement—your clear and concise expectations of their performance, what a win looks like. If you are vague in any critical area it is bound to show up when you least expect or desire to see it. It is hard to be positive and aggressive if you are confused about what is expected.

A Performance Review—a periodic review of individual and team performance, are we on target? If not, what adjustments are needed? Poorly designed or communicated performance agreements result in disappointment and need rewritten. If performance agreements are well written and both parties actually agree, the review is simply that—a review, not a meeting full of surprises.

A Performance Management—the process of using a well-written performance agreement and a strong partnership in the performance review producing a superior performance on a regular basis. Most people do not want managed but most want to fulfill their leader's expectations—please, do not make it a guessing game.

Great leaders help their team members, individually and as a team reach their full potential. They use on-going feedback and dialogue in clarifying winning expectations. If you measure performance expectations against your mission, vision, values and stated goals, you gain maximum potential.

Clarity about individual and team performance always contributes in achieving organizational and leadership strategies eliminating surprises and disappointments.

"For I know the thoughts that I think toward you, says the Lord, thoughts of peace and not evil, to give you a future and a hope" —Jeremiah 29:11.

No leader I know comes close to being God, though some act as if they were, all leaders should give their people hope for a better future—fulfilled expectations.

I have heard it said, "If everything is important, then nothing is important." Every morning leader's wake up to a multitude of details and responsibilities I liken to facing a herd of gorillas. How you handle your daily concerns and unanticipated distractions determines your level of success and effectiveness.

The key to managing this challenge is identifying the 3-5 issues that have the greatest return on your time, energy, and resources. Once identified, spend all your time and energy focused on those issues, defer, delegate, or eliminate the rest.

When asked, what should core leaders focus on and why? I always respond, "All successful organizations focus first on being healthy and second being smarter."

Organizations demonstrate they are healthy by

They eliminate politics, pettiness, confusion, and all other forms of emotional immaturity. This act alone leads to higher team morale, longevity, and greater productivity. There is a prevailing culture of value and concern for every team member, higher energy and broader engagement by the team, and a rising spirit of faith for the future.

Everyone operates with a spirit of abundance, there is plenty for everyone, and not a spirit of lack, no hoarders allowed.

A spirit of excellence permeates every aspect of every detail, every day, by every team member, every time. Leaders, at every level, are passionate about developing future leaders and building effective teams. They do not succumb to fads, but understand the importance of staying current, relevant, and resonant.

Healthy organizations have a way of getting smarter, while unhealthy organizations, regardless of how smart, die every day. Great leaders spend 80% of their time helping organizations get healthier and hire managers to get them smarter.

Day 3
Attracting, Developing, and Retaining

When leaders focus more on getting smarter instead of healthier, it may indicate they are avoiding the realities of human behavior required for getting healthier. Realities such as brutal honesty with present reality, discipline, and courage—all are critical in facing emotional immaturity, number one challenge in the workplace.

Attracting, developing, and retaining mature qualified people are the passion and priority of healthy organizations and their leaders. Turing them into a passionate winning team is their number two priority. This passion is the most critical of the four passions because it is the key to success for the other three. It is also the most difficult because:

The core essence of attracting good people and building great teams is—trust, time consuming to build and can be lost in one conversation. Politics (humanness) is the greatest hindrance to building an effective leadership team. Politics is the result of unresolved personal issues at all levels of organizational life. Attempting to cure political issues without addressing the source, senior leadership, is pointless.

How do you recognize a dream team?

They are passionate about every detail, being productive every day, and never idle, exhausting, or boring. Their meetings are compelling forums for asking well thought out and many times, difficult questions, and tackling the tough ones first.

They have no problem challenging any idea, but passionately support the final decision regardless of who brings it forward. They hold each other accountable for behaviors that are not conducive for effective team performance and sacrifice personal preference for the good of the team.

How do you build a dream team? The most important activity is building relational equity in an atmosphere of trust as a way of life, not an occasional event. This involves being honest with yourself and everyone else.

My experience indicates that a team's relational effectiveness has greater impact on their chance for success than its collective experience, knowledge, or talent. Cohesiveness at the senior leadership level is the **number one indicator** of future success any organization can achieve.

Day 4
What Did You Expect?

Well, what did you expect?" People operate and perform based on their own worldview. In absence of your clear expectations, they create their own. If I have heard it once, I have heard it a thousand times, "I'm not sure what's expected or I assumed you wanted ..." Great leaders never assume and never launch a day, much less a new initiative, until they know everyone knows the goals and expectations.

Poor performance, team members quitting, conflict, and lack of energy and engagement - reads like a checklist of any leaders worst headache. Whilst there is no one-size-fits-all solution, I have found one common denominator—unclear or mismatched expectations. Your purpose and expectations, for yourself and for your team, must be clear and without question. They must be more than fancy plaques, framed mission and vision statements, and a list of goals on a wall chart in the boardroom.

However, you communicate your purpose and performance expectations, the following fundamental questions need clarity in the mind of your team:

Who are we?
Why do we exist?
What do we do?
Why do we do it?
How do we measure success?

Do not start your day or allow your teams start their day without knowing the answers to those questions.

Seven steps for improving performance expectations:

Make them clear in your mind, otherwise, how do you explain your confusion or hesitation to your team? Expectations should always be about filling the "gaps"—your team know where they are, and are they passionate about filling them?

Everyone must understand "the why," not just "what" and how. Few people are passionate about just knowing what to do and how to do it; they must see the greater purpose and their personal connection to the outcome.

Meet and discuss, but only after you complete steps one through three, if you do, your meetings are redundant at best, and worse, pointless and a waste of everyone's time.

Once your team has clarity on the above fundamental questions, make the performance expectations an agreement—not your personal edict or command. Write the performance agreement, not as a legal document or condition of employment, but a goal both parties agree with and work together to achieve.

Celebrate small wins along the way—do not wait to throw a big party at the end. Watch for diminishing efforts and find something to celebrate.

Once your team knows the answer to "well, what did you expect," and assured of your emotional and practical support, you can expect higher energy, more engagement on a daily basis, and frequent success—I guarantee it!

Day 5
You Cannot Over Communicate

Whether it is a slip of the tongue or a big ole foot-in-the-mouth moment, communication blunders happen to the best of us. What is important beyond doing damage control, is that we learn from our mistakes, even better, learn from others' mistakes. Saturation communication is the mantra of all successful organizations.

In Spartanburg, South Carolina, Michele Bachman, congressional representative running for president, urged the crowd to join her in celebrating Elvis Presley's birthday. Thinking this would be a great applause line she was stunned by the lack of response. Turns out that August 16, the date of her speech, was not the Rock and Roll King's birthday, it was the date of his death 34 years earlier. Lesson: check your facts, especially if you practice "saturation communication."

Once your organization is clear about its purpose, expectations, roles, and goals—get everyone in a spirit of agreement and their efforts aligned to the goals through saturation communication. You can overload people with information but you can never over-communicate. Use every means possible to communicate until everyone "speaks the same language."

Keep three things in mind when communicating

1. Repetition is still the greatest teacher, do not get bored or weary repeating key messages.

2. Simplicity, K.I.S.S., "Keep it Simple Stupid." The more complicated the message—the greater potential for confusion, misinformation, and rumor.
3. Multiple mediums: use a wide variety of communication methods with your people. Assumption is life's lowest level of knowledge

Learn, develop, and practice consistently the "circle of communication," keep communicating until the message returns to the originator. At the end of every meeting, answer the question: "What do we need to communicate to our team members?" Time spent clarifying issues and practicing saturation communication is time well spent.

How do you know if your organization practices saturation?

Ask front-line team members if they know why the organization exists? What are our fundamental values? What action plan do we have in place to fulfill our mission? What are our goals for this year and what is our strategy to reach them?

How does your role and efforts affect each question?

Blank stares and incorrect answers are good indicators more accurate, adequate, and shared information is needed. Passionate effort and engagement is always preceded by passionate, consistent, and saturated communication.

Verbally telling and disseminating information through emails, and social media is not communicating and listening does not always understand. Until both parties agree on what message was sent, appropriate is action taken, you have not communicated.

Day 6
Five Things Leaders Never Compromise

Compromise, is it a leadership strength or weakness? According to Dictionary.com, the word compromise means, "a settlement of differences by mutual concessions; an agreement reached by adjustment of conflicting or opposing claims and principles by reciprocal modification of demands."

In Steven Covey's book, "The Third Alternative," Covey contrasts compromise and synergy. He illustrates Compromise as -1+1 = 1.5 and Synergy as -1+1 = 3. Covey adds, "Do you catch yourself agreeing to compromise simply because you don't want to invest the time and effort to create synergy, or because the other person won't pursue synergy with you?"

Leaders must lead and sometimes the only way of moving forward within the available time constraints is compromise—but never at the expense of essential principles, trust, and integrity. Compromise is a management tool used often, but rarely used by leaders. Great leaders never leave problems unresolved or team members frustrated by kicking the can down the road through compromise.

Five things great leaders never compromise

1. Maintaining the balance between pursuing the vision with passion, developing their core leaders' fullest potential, and managing the team's mission responsibly.

2. Developing a saturation communication and wise decision-making culture through accurate, adequate and shared information; coupled with open, honest, and collaborative conversations.

3. Staying engaged with their team; mentally, emotionally, and spiritually while remaining focused on enlarging the team's leadership capacity and capability.

4. Mobilizing and enlarging the team's vision through a resonant, shared, and resourced purpose.

5. They model and keep the team's shared value system—the motivation and inspiration for creating a productive working and serving environment.

Compromise is neither a strength nor weakness, but a tool great leader's only use until they find a way to create a "win-win" solution, no one loses. In a compromise, everyone loses something and the best decisions seldom made.

Day 7
Self-Awareness: A Discipline Of Great Leaders

Four plaques have hung in my office for years with the following sayings:

"The quality of a person's life is their commitment to excellence regardless of their chosen field of endeavor."
—Vince Lombardi

"In the middle of every difficulty lies opportunity."
—Albert Einstein.

"The pessimist sees the difficulty in every opportunity; the optimist sees the opportunity in *every difficulty.*"
—*Winston Churchill*

"Things come to those who wait but only things left by those who hustle."
—*Abraham Lincoln*

SELF-AWARENESS, it protects you from being self-absorbed and merely role driven. Self-examination is a way of life for all great leaders—"let a man examine himself." Your life experience should be the integration of your God-given mission, talent and personality.

Self-awareness includes

Self-knowledge: knowing WHO you are is paramount for success.

Self-mindedness: knowing your motives and why you do things will increase effectiveness.

Self-vigilance: knowing what makes you tick and what ticks you and others off helps you avoid conflicts.

Self-consciousness: knowing how you come across to others and then regulating your interactions.

Self-alertness: maintaining your emotional, physical, mental and spiritual condition.

When thinking of yourself keep in mind Romans 12:3 where the Apostle Paul said, "For by the grace given to me I say to every one of you not to think more highly of yourself than you ought to think, but to think with sober judgment as God has distributed to each of you a measure of faith."

For years, I have heard well-meaning people define humility as, "Not thinking of yourself and more of others, but not thinking of yourself at all." That sounds pious but it is not biblical and has been the downfall of many.

Without a clear and honest understanding of yourself, you never develop healthy relationships. It is because Jesus knew WHO he was he had no problem washing the feet of his disciples, because he knew who created the bodies to which they were attached.

Great leaders have no problem serving those who serve them because through a lifetime of self-examination they have a healthy understanding of their own strengths and weaknesses and know how to serve with true humility and not from a position of superiority.

Day 8
7 Things Core Values Do For You

1. They reveal your DNA, not what makes you better but the values that make you different. Most conflicts in any organization, regardless of kind, size, and leadership are a values issue when its all said and done.
2. They make decision-making easier for team members when the leader is away. You eliminate 75% of wasted time and needless discussions when there is consensus and passion about the same core values.
3. They help determine who joins your team. Most of the time, the wrong people end up on your team because little thought and effort was given to the core values before the hiring decision is made.
4. They help determine who leaves your team. If you have frustration with present team members, I would bet the farm it is over values. Clarity about core values takes precedent over ability, personality, and performance when deciding to release a person.
5. They create the culture or environment that nurtures your mission, vision and strategy. Stress, lack of energy and participation, turnover rate, and a lot of other issues are traced back to a lack of understanding and commitment to core values.
6. They help create the scorecard for your team members' performance agreement and performance review. Passionate buy in to the organization's core values always reflects in performance and production.
7. They aid great leaders' daily and future decisions affecting everyone. Every decision must be consistent

with your core values or you confuse and de-energize your team.

Day 9
7 Ways To Leverage Your Leadership Influence

1. Start a "To stop doing list." Twenty percent of your efforts produce eighty percent of your best results. Focus more on the twenty percent and delegate the eighty percent.
2. Determine your personal, family and calling values—protect them at all costs. Values are 5-7 things you never compromise. Learn to say NO more often; others' emergency should not always be your urgency.
3. Practice Luke 2:52 daily. Keep growing in wisdom, favor with God and man, and take care of the only temple you will ever have. Without them, you leverage very little.
4. Be average, be good and be great. Average (competent) in everything relating to your destiny, consistently good in the things necessary to fulfill your goals, and great in the one thing God has gifted and called you to accomplish.
5. Get better at leading your own life. Have a tool that manages the events and activities creating the demand on your time, energy and resources. Think leverage and advantage—not businesses and quantity.
6. Develop people and build teams. Leverage your influence helping others reach their goals and realize their dreams. Increased synergy and momentum for your vision comes through leveraging your team - not you working harder on the task.
7. Seek His Kingdom first—Matthew 6:33. You keep your priorities straight. If you do not, your followers get

confused about what is important and end up leveraging the trivial and neglecting the important.

Day 10
10 Keys To Overcoming Difficult Times

Someone once said, "If you ain't in over your head, how do you know how tall you are?" It is not if difficult times come, they come to everyone, it's what you do with them when they come that matters. How you handle adversity determines the strength and value of your leadership. Tough times do more to strengthen your inner resolve than good times ever will.

10 keys that have helped me overcome

1. Acknowledge and accept present reality and take personal responsibility.
2. Seek help if you sense immediate and serious danger.
3. Protect your health—mentally, physically, socially, and spiritually.
4. Get to the root of the difficulty—stop dealing only with the symptoms.
5. Declare your intent to be accountable outside of yourself.
6. Control your confession—your words are powerful.
7. Enlist support, build a team, and quit being a hero.
8. Set goals and track your progress—daily.
9. Know how to handle, learn from, and leverage your setbacks.
10. Lighten up, laugh and develop a merry heart.

Great leaders make the best of difficult times before difficult times take the best from them. They do not feel sorry for themselves, do not let people live in their minds rent free, embrace change—not resist it, and do not focus on things out of their control.

"I hated every minute of training, but I said, don't quit, suffer now and love the rest of your life as a champion." — Mohammad Ali

Day 11
Identifying, Attracting And retaining The Best People

During good or bad economic times, a sound system for identifying, attracting and retaining the best team members is a priority for all above average organizations.

Allowing the wrong person to join your team is not only frustrating for everyone but costs financially and wastes a lot of time and energy.

All great organizations have a solid recruiting strategy that includes at least the following five steps:

1. **Define the organization:** Communicate who you are (your culture) not just what you do. As great as you think your organization is—it is not a good fit for everyone. People who think they fit everywhere usually create the most disappointment.

2. **Define the role:** Future team members should know what their role is and is not. Create a clear job description and performance agreement, the details of what they do and what a winning performance looks like. Do them it well—it is your first impression to potential team members.

3. **Develop a marketing campaign:** Finding the right team member is just as important as finding the right client or customer. Word of mouth and personal recommendations are good but can also put a leader in an uncomfortable position when hiring out of obligation or as a personal favor.

4.   **Develop of selection process:** Do not proceed without a systematic detailed selection process after you have narrowed the field. Determine in advance what questions are asked and by whom. Avoid bias and stereotyping based on physical appearance or other factors. Look beyond their *"package"* and resume, they can be deceiving—positive or negative. Remember, certain questions are off limits in today's marketplace environment.

5.   **Administer background and reference checks:** It has proven costly and disappointing to make assumptions—including a person's honesty. Resumes have a tendency to embellish and you rarely find a potential candidate gives you a reference that speaks to their weaknesses--and everyone has a few.

Create consensus on a potential candidate. Have at least three mature team members who will work with the new person, interview the candidate, if it is only informally. They do not make the final decision, but they can give you a feel for the chemistry. They will work for you but they will work with the team. You do not want to have to *"sell"* them on the organization and then have to sell them to the team, let your core leaders participate in the process up front.

Remember, be slow to appoint so you do not have to disappoint. There is one thing worse than having a vacancy; it is having the wrong person filling it. Now you have two problems; you still do not have the right team member and you have the wrong person you have to release.

Day 12
Winners & Losers vs. Winners & Learners

Some years ago, IBM had a junior executive that made a tactical error costing the company $9 million. The following week the young man was called to the CEO's office thinking he would be fired. Instead, the Chairman began discussing plans for a new project, which he wanted the young executive to direct.

Feeling uncomfortable, the young man interrupted the Chairman: "Excuse me sir, you know I just cost the company $9 million why are you putting me in charge? I thought I came here today to be fired." The Chairman responded, "I've just invested $9 million educating you, you're now one of my most valuable assets."

Great leaders constantly look for winners among the learners. Poor leaders throw away what they perceive as losers looking for a winner. Great leaders see conflict and mistakes as possibilities to learn, poor leaders see them as problems to solve.

Your attitude colors your thoughts and your leadership approach. Most young, immature, and inexperienced leaders are unaware of how their negative thoughts and actions shape their worldview and influence their teams' attitude and success.

There are two dramatically contrasting attitudes that can shape your leadership—Perfection vs. Discovery. Perfection says, "Is this good enough?" It is usually not. Discovery says, "What's good here, and can we do it better?"

The search for perfection sets up winners and losers. The conversation involves questions and issues such as: who's right and who's wrong, why mistakes are unacceptable, judgmental and non-negotiable attitudes prevail, everyone's

playing the blame game instead of accepting responsibility, and the willingness to take risks and innovate is non-existent. The steam is gone from any self-esteem that may be left.

On the other-hand, the process of discovery creates a culture of winners and learners. There are no "failures"--only learning opportunities. Self-esteem and value stay elevated in an atmosphere of hope.

Mistakes need corrected and errors avoided, but not at the expense stifling peoples' creative juices and innovative spirit. Great leaders never throw caution to the wind, but neither do they discourage the willingness to step into the unknown and find a new path. If they do, they can kiss their most gifted, motivated, and profitable team members good-bye.

Life is not about winning and losing - it is about learning whether you win or lose. The essence of great leadership is more than picking winners and losers, any Leadership 101 graduate can do that, it is finding winners among the learners.

Day 13
Why Some Teams Work And Others Do Not

"Teams have been studied to death in recent years and the verdict is in. Some are a success and some are a disaster. Few are in the middle. The key is how they are led and how they are managed and whether senior leaders really support them." —J. Richard Hackman, Harvard University.

Most of the time when teams or individuals are not producing well, the team leader is the problem. Since most team leaders are really managers, disguised as a leader, they commit two common errors. First, they act like a boss, telling everyone what to do and how to do it, or second, they think they have empowered the team, but in reality, they have abandoned the team.

Five Problems Common to All Teams

1. Unhealthy conflict evidenced by personal attacks, sarcasm, lack of support, and aggressive behavior. Remedy: Clarify the issue immediately and confront if necessary, focus on behavior and stop attacking people's character or personality, create a plan for healthy conflict resolution.
2. They have trouble in reaching consensus on key issues, evidenced by rigid positions and opinions, and have the same old arguments with no new information or solutions offered. Remedy: Find small agreements, ask what it will take to agree, and discuss the outcomes if the lack of compromise continues.

3. Communication failure, evidenced by members constantly interrupting and talking over one another, others will not talk at all, and everyone dances around the real issues. Remedy: Create norms for discussions, actively solicit other views and consider outside coaching.

4. There is lack of progress, evidenced by assignments not completed or frequently not on time, poor participation levels, and low engagement and energy at meetings. Remedy: Provide clear assignments and performance agreements, challenging but reachable goals, and productive debriefings outlining cause and effect results.

5. Poor leadership, evidenced by leaders acting like a one-man show, the leader is a poor delegator, poorly defined mission, vision, values and strategy, and the leader has no apparent team-building skills. Remedy: Find a new leader and allow the current one to manage what he does best. If the current leader has leadership potential, put him or her on a development track before assigning them to another team.

What makes you a good team member will hurt you as a team leader unless you make the proper adjustments. Some great people are never able to make the move from being a team member to being a team leader; they are great producers as team member but fail in getting the team to produce.

Day 14
Set a Goal and Work Hard or Work Hard and Hope

"Of all the things I've done, the most vital is coordinating those who work with me and aiming their efforts at a certain goal."—Walt Disney.

The purpose of setting goals is moving your team to accomplish more through focused efforts.

You seldom hit poorly defined targets. Unless you have unlimited resources, your job as a leader is to focus your limited resources, including personnel and on the things that matter most. As a leader, stewardship of all your resources is your number one responsibility.

Effective goals: are recognized and supported by all team members; clear and easy to understand; written and specific; measurable with time constraints; aligned with organizational strategy; challenging but achievable, and rewarded appropriately.

Most inexperienced or poorly led organizations make three common mistakes. First, they set no goals or goals poorly thought through and managed. Second, they fail to create performance measurements that provide objective evidence of progress and achievement. Third, they fail to align goals to the organization's strategy and provide appropriate rewards.

Goals should be a combination of top down, bottom up, and all around. Top leaders need to take the lead in setting overall goals for the organization, but encourage input from the front-line team members. Every team member needs to set their own goals based on the organizational goals.

Interrelated departments should complement each other's goals and not build personal silos.

Goals have four key components to be effective: (1) break each goal into specific tasks; (2) plan the execution strategy; (3) gather adequate resources; (4) execute the plan. When you prioritize goals, everything goal cannot be number one. Focus the efforts of your best people and the lion's share of your resources on goals that bring the best return on investment.

Be results oriented, celebrate every goal reached, and learn from every experience—no effort is minor or without consequence.

"God, who is eternally complete, who directs the stars, who is the master of fates, who elevates man from his lowliness to Himself, who speaks from the cosmos to every single human soul, is the most brilliant manifestation of the goal of perfection." —Alfred Adler

Day 15
Leveraging Your Leadership Influence

"If women realized what influence they really had, they would be filled with pride. If men recognized how influential women are, they would be scared to death." –Katherine Kehler

It's been said that we all influence at least 250 people in our lifetime. Most people, including leaders, underestimate their influence. Mother Teresa was a great humanitarian in India and one of the most influential women of the 20th Century. Madonna, a racy rock star, had fame—Mother Teresa had greatness. Both influenced millions but in entirely different ways, one temporal the other eternal. Leadership is all about leveraging your influence.

Here are seven passions all great leaders use to leverage their leadership influence:

1. The passion for knowledge and truth. Great leadership begins with an awareness of the facts and a wide range of information. Facts help you deal with present reality but a revelation of the Truth prepares you for the unknown future.

2. The passion for wisdom. Discipline comes because of knowing the facts and acting on them, wisdom understands how to use them wisely. Excellence is not a goal but a way of life built on God-honoring standards and principles learned only by a passion for wisdom.

3. The passion for discernment and discretion. Decisions based on wise discernment and discretion determines your future. You make decisions every day that affect

your health, finances, and family, emotional and spiritual well-being.

4. The passion for honesty and integrity. In today's culture we do not lie, we miss-speak. Telling the truth is honesty, telling it all the time is integrity. *"The words of the godly lead to life; evil people cover up their harmful intentions."* Proverbs 9:11

5. The passion for humility. The balance for strength in leadership and humbleness in attitude is a constant battle for most people. Pretending to be strong or humble will not fill the gaps in your leadership. Only awareness plus action, based on humility fills the gap.

6. The passion for spiritual discipline and surrender. We often hear about self-discipline, but without spiritual maturity, it often leads to self-destruction and dozens of personality disorders so prevalent today. Maybe that is why 80% of Americans are using some kind of mood or mind-altering drug.

7. The passion to live within reasonable limits in every area of life including health, finances, and relationships. Learning to live within your limits while serving an unlimited God is what separates great leaders from all the rest. Never limit God but never over run your own - it's called Wisdom!

No one ever leveraged his leadership influence more than Jesus Christ of Nazareth when he took twelve average marketplace people, formed them into a team, ignited their passion for a cause, and leveraged that into a force that turned their world upside down.

Day 16
Seven Keys to a Good Strategic Plan

Leaders who say they have vision but cannot define it, have no plan to get there always amaze me. Until there are values that create a healthy work environment, goals to keep the team focused, and an action plan to guide the journey— you do not have a vision you simply have an idea.

Strategic planning brings objectivity and structure to the planning process. It provides a road map for success. Strategic planning directs the investment of resources and provides accountability for results. It is the only way to measure success and return on investment.

Good strategic plans, properly executed include the following:

1. Clarifies your mission, vision and values statements.
2. Improves the decision-making process.
3. Anticipates and productively manages change.
4. Aligns personal and team priorities.
5. Establishes performance expectations.
6. Analyzes your systems and processes.
7. Creates and maintains a culture of continued improvement.

Do you have a vision or just a good idea? A good idea without goals and an action plan make for a good discussion but produces very little action or significant and sustainable results.

Day 17
What's the Turnover Rate on Your Team?

"Immediate supervisors trump the best organizations. It is not that employee-focused initiatives are unimportant—it is just your immediate supervisor is more important. They define and pervade your work environment. If the relationship with your leader is fractured, then no amount of in-chair massaging or company-sponsored dog walking will persuade you to stay and perform. It's better to work for a great leader in an old-fashioned company than for a terrible manager in an enlightened, company-focused culture." –Marcus Buckingham

Finding and keeping great team members are two sides of the same coin. Some organizations have set up an Office of Retention reporting directly to the CEO. Others have instituted work-life balance programs designed to relieve stress at home. Casual dress, on-site childcare, brings your pet day, and a plethora of other efforts trying to retain good people.

Keeping your best talent is not just a "feel good" issue or always money related. Volumes of books are written on why it's important to keep people; losing intellectual talent, cost of recruiting and training new people, more work for remaining team members, morale tanks, customers wondering why your good people are leaving, and a dozen other reasons.

People stay with you for a few basic reasons. First, they want to work with well-led and managed organizations. Second, they respect their direct supervisor. Third, they are fairly compensated, not only wages and benefits, but opportunities to grow personally and professionally. Fourth, the chance to work with respected, compatible and motivated team members. Fifth, their work is challenging, satisfying and stimulating.

Why do good people leave? First, the quality of top leaders shifts or declines. Second, unreasonable conflicts arise with immediate supervisors. Third, close friends' leave taking away a meaningful affiliation. Fourth, unfavorable change of responsibilities occurs. The work no longer appealing or their abilities do not match their responsibilities. Fifth, problems with work-life balance happening beyond their ability to change.

Great leaders have a low turnover rate because they know to attract good people, care for their as team members, and put them ahead of customer satisfaction. They take such good care of all their people—it makes leaving difficult.

The turnover rate on your team is a key indicator of the effectiveness of your leadership, your ability to attract good people, develop them, and build a team. It has little to do with your education, intellect, and organizational skills.

Day 18
Problem Team Members--Ignore, Develop or Release?

When Phil Jackson, NBA title-winning coach of the Chicago Bulls, talks about how he handled Dennis Rodman, a rule breaking out of control player of the 90s, he said he managed to gain control by giving it up—at least in the mind of Rodman. Jackson explained, *"When we try to control to control the actions of independent-minded, highly paid talents, it's like putting cattle in a small pasture, they keep breaking through the fence."*

Every organization has "A" players, their performance and attitude are outstanding, "B" players, their performance is average to good and "C" players, and their performance ranges from barely acceptable to *"this person has to go."* Poor leaders cater to the "A" players, load up the "B's" and cover for the "C's" until they can find a legal reason to fire them.

Great leaders facilitate the "A" players, nurture the "B's" and find creative ways to move the "C's" up a level, if possible. The cost of replacing a problem team member may cost you more than devising a plan to improve their performance or many times, they leave willingly at no cost or discomfort to you or the team.

Before replacing problem people make sure you make a reasonable investment in making them a viable team member, especially if you invested heavily in the potential you saw when you asked them to join your team. Remember, be slow in appointing to avoid disappointing.

Poor leaders try motivating problem people, most of the time without any significant or sustainable success. Our English word, **motivation** comes from two Latin words meaning, *"To come from behind and push."* It is difficult motivating anyone to do anything for very long when there is no inner desire to improve, not even more money.

Motivation is a personal decision that only individuals can make based on their internal *motivators*. Keep in mind, there are as many motivational factors as there are people - do not spend much time figuring it out, they have it or they do not.

Great leaders inspire properly motivated team members. They deal with motivation factors first and production expectations second. Some keys to working with poorly motivated people are; pay attention early and often, identify and address any work-life balance issues, make sure they understand their assignment and expectations, and finally is your leadership the problem?

Most people are not *"bad people"* by nature, they may have a key that you or other supervisors have overlooked, ignored or refused to develop. *"Bad-boy"* Dennis Rodman joined Michael Jordan, the consummate professional, and performed admirably helping the team win six NBA championships.

Day 19
A 15-minnute Vision Checkup

Ask your core leaders these seven questions. If they answer no or show any hesitation, plan a "vision day" ASAP. If your core leaders show doubt, rest assured your team members on the front line do not have a clue.

1. *IMAGINABLE*—does our vision convey a compelling picture of our future?
2. *DESIRABLE*—does our vision grab and keep the attention of at least two generations?
3. *FEASIBLE*—is our vision built on reasonable, stretchable, and achievable goals?
4. *FOCUSED*—does our vision guide and dominate our decision making process?
5. *FLEXIBLE*—does our vision allow for individual creativity, innovation and changing conditions?
6. *COMMUNICABLE*—can all core leaders "tell our story" and cast our vision in 100 words or less?
7. *EXECUTABLE*—is our strategy well-conceived understood and embraced by all the team members?

If you and your team cannot answer with certainty these, your leadership influence questionable at and suspect at worst. Find someone else to manage and you work on getting the "message" found in these seven questions across to your team.

If you don't you will find yourself chasing an undefined dream, leading a team that hasn't a clue how to help you, and you are not sure about empowering them.

Day 20
Why Don't People Follow You?

A compelling vision is like a trailer for a blockbuster movie. A 30-minute clip highlights the movie and compels you to watch the entire story. Like a movie trailer, the vision keeps you focused on your dream and doing whatever it takes to see it happen.

Many organizational vision statements are like a "B"-rated movie; the plot is vague, the acting is second-rate, you regret buying the ticket regardless of how cheap and the whole experience drains your energy—sound familiar?

Only "*sick people*" sit through a bad movie twice, yet this describes the daily experience of millions of team members who sit through second-rate leadership visions simply because they need the job. Is your team following you because your vision is compelling or because you hand them a check every week?

Your vision is a picture of everyone's hoped-for result: what the end looks like, what we produce, and how we function every day. Does everyone on your team *"see"* the same thing, work toward the same goal, and operate with the same values?

The vision must not only resonate with you but with everyone following you, if not, conflict, confusion, and unfulfilled dreams are in your future. The vision must reach your teams' inner aspirations, its language translates into a realistic strategy, and its fulfillment challenging, but achievable.

If you want an energized team, following you your vision must be clear, compelling, and easy to explain. Even if implementing your vision is complicated, explaining it should not be. Your vision cannot be abstract or vague and compelling at the same time.

If you want your team excited about the future, show it to them often until your vision becomes *"our vision."*

"The greatest achievement was at first and for a time a dream. The oak sleeps in the acorn, the bird waits in the egg, and in the highest vision of the soul, a waking angel stirs. Dreams are the seedlings of realities." James Allen

What embryonic dream rests in your heart waiting to birth into a compelling vision that causes others to follow for no other reason than seeing the dream become a reality?

People following you only for a check, a perk or a position never help you fulfill your vision—instead they greatly hinder your chances.

Day 21
12 Reasons Why Strategic Planning is so Important

1. Provides a common purpose and platform for teamwork.
2. Prioritizes the use of resources, facilities/equipment, personal & finances.
3. Provides a tool for measuring success.
4. Brings clarity on mission, vision, and values.
5. Helps leaders anticipate and manage change and solve problems.
6. It keeps organizations looking through the telescope and not just the microscope.
7. Improves the decision-making in quality and success and rate.
8. Aligns leaders, staff, and stakeholders.
9. Establishes expectations for everyone.
10. Keeps systems and processes in a constant state of review.
11. Identifies organizational strengths and weaknesses.
12. Establishes a culture of continuous improvement.

Activity without an action plan may produce perspiration but without a strategy, it produces very little inspiration and hardly any sustainable results. If your front-line team members do not know the mission and the plan to finish it how do they passionately provide excellence in service?

Day 22
Are You an Asset or Liability?

When you walk into the lobby of the ServiceMaster headquarters building in Downers Grove, Illinois you see on your right a curving marble wall that stretches ninety feet and stands eighteen feet tall. Carved prominently in that stonewall in letters four feet high are their four corporate values:

1. To Honor God in all we do
2. To help people develop
3. To pursue excellence
4. To grow profitably

Is it any wonder then that return on equity has averaged 50 percent and stock values have grown in value from one dollar per share to over twenty-eight dollars per share? That kind of sustained performance does not happen unless God and people are assets to be esteemed and not *"tools"* to be used for turning a profit or personal ambition.

In today's America God and people are quickly becoming liabilities and no longer assets. When ServiceMaster first established their corporate values and made them prominent, it raised eyebrows. The critics asked, *"Aren't you on shaky ground when you try to mix God and profits? And what about employees who don't choose to behave the way you do--aren't you forcing your religious beliefs on them?"*

We live and work (minister) in a pluralistic society where many question the very existence of God and our right as believers to represent Him in the marketplace. When determining whether you are an asset or a liability keeps in context, which Kingdom comes first—the secular kingdoms of this earth or the Kingdom of Light—one is temporal, the other is eternal. I believe you must be an asset to both but for different reasons.

In your drive to be an asset in today's marketplace, which gives you the platform to represent the Kingdom of Light, don't allow your work environment be emasculated to a neutrality of no belief at best, or worse, one of disbelief. You are an asset to your workplace when you add to the bottom line profits. You are an asset to the Kingdom of Light when you live your faith, without apology, in a way that honors God and adds value and dignity to your team members. *"For even I (Jesus) came to earth not to be served but to serve others and give my life as a ransom for many"* Mark 10:45. Anyone with a servant's heart is an asset to any company and certainly to God's kingdom. Christians do a lot of damage when they try to be an asset in God's kingdom but are a liability to the company in which they represent Him.

Day 23
You Want the Truth—You can't Handle the Truth

Most movie buffs recognize this line from the movie *"A Few Good Men"* spoken by Jack Nicolson to a young Tom Cruise. Great leaders help their team deal with the truth with brutal honesty. No team is ready to move forward, regardless how gifted and skilled, until this becomes a way of life and not an occasional exercise.

Assessing the truth about the non-human elements of your organization is usually a straightforward academic exercise. Difficulty comes when dealing with the perceptions and emotions of the live humans making up your team about the facts undergirding everyone's perception of those facts.

Teamwork becomes a problem when there is strong disagreement about the distance between the world as everyone thinks it is, how everyone thinks it should be, and the way the facts say it is. Great leaders know how to bring all three world's into focus while maintaining the peace and advancing the vision.

Great leadership is more than accumulating the facts; it is developing a team out of very diverse and gifted individuals who have learned how to handle each other's perceptions of the Truth with emotional maturity. Only mature leaders, regardless of position or title, can accomplish that task.

Day 24
Don't Drain Your Team's Energy

Be careful your leadership does not drain the energy out of your team. Creating energy seldom means pep talks, hype and painting inspirational word pictures of what could be. Energy and inspiration for the future comes from being brutally honest about present reality and a determination that it is not going to stay that way.

Great leaders through their attitude, articulation, actions and reactions bring life and energy on a daily basis. It is more than having an upbeat personality, wearing smile on your face by walking through the closet last night and got a coat hanger stuck in your mouth.

Great leaders believe in their mission and vision. They are absolutely certain God has picked them to lead and they make no compromises in surrounding themselves with like-minded team members. They do not have a messiah complex believing they must have all the answers and solving all the problems.

They are real people; reflect a servant's heart in all they do, and willing to "get in the trenches with their team. They make asking questions a leadership style and not just a way to get information. They are quicker to allow others to find their own answers than always handing out solutions.

When you walk into a room or situation, do you increase the energy or de-energize it? Are you known as a hope-dealer or dream-killer? You team has enough other issues that drain their energy, don't you be another one.

Day 25
Stop Look and Listen—Before Releasing a Team Member

Before releasing Vision-*Drainers*, great leaders do the following three things:

1. Describe what you have observed in their behavior. Be fair and honest without being judgmental. Show what needs to improve and why.

2. Be clear about what is acceptable. Give additional teaching and training if necessary. Remember, no amount of teaching or training can make up for a poor attitude or non-productive behavior. Trying to lead or coach vision-drainers is frustrating and a team-spirit killer if continued very long.

3. Make sure they understand the consequences of continued poor performance and set a deadline for improvement. Have them summarize your conversation and commit to making the needed changes.

Winning and losing is first an attitude before it is an action or an outcome. No one is blessed with all Vision-Makers—not even Jesus. However, He did turn many losers into winners because of His attitude toward them. Talk about a great leader!

Day 26
Building Creative, Unified and Loyal Teams

Selecting, developing and empowering the right people are only half the leadership challenge in building a team. Leading them to leverage their skills, individual egos and emotions as team to accomplish the mission is the other half. Some leaders are good at one or the other. A few are good at both model your leadership after them.

Great leaders know they can take average performers with impeccable character and the heart of a team player and get above average results. There is no such thing as the perfect team. Ideal conditions, unlimited resources and team members who never disappoint do not exist. The ultimate success or failure of any effort is determined by leadership's ability to build great teams—not perfect teams.

Seven steps great leaders use in building great teams:

1. Don't make changes to just make a mark for yourself or build your reputation. If the change does not make the team better, do not make it until it does.
2. Be approachable and generous with information and challenging opportunities. This makes great people eager to join your team.
3. Maintain a well-ordered environment so everyone knows where he or she stands and what is expected.
4. Break down hierarchies, cliques and silo-builders that hinder a team spirit and teamwork. Cross training always helps.

5. Be fair and impartial when giving out compensation, workloads, and corrections. Imbalance makes everyone feel uncomfortable.

6. Lead by example. The higher your leadership position simply means your mop bucket is bigger. You are not paid to use it on a regular basis but occasionally it helps. Shows you value everyone on your team and respect his or her contribution.

7. Have opportunities for relationship building outside the task or job location. Your team members need to relate to you and each other as friends - not just colleagues.

Day 27
Building Relational Equity

Building great teams through relational equity and vision is not accomplished by inspirational speaking but passionate listing. You must understand the hearts and minds of those you lead if you want to keep their hands and feet for the long haul or during tough times.

Tone-deaf leaders create negative emotions, confusion and eventually discord and strife. Ask questions, listen with your heart, provide support, develop skills, create agreement and above all—make emotional connections.

How you view people is how you treat people. If you view them as your helpers instead of you being their facilitator you tend to use people, not empower them. You must listen with your heart and not just your head. Most accomplished leaders can out talk someone but most never try to "out listen"—try it, that is how you help most people and build the most relational equity from which future demands are covered.

Day 28
Can Your Team Answer the Following Questions?

Leader, if you and your team cannot answer the following questions, the success of your mission is doubtful and probably not worth anyone's best effort:

1. Mission—why do we exist?
2. Vision—what do we want to be?
3. Core values—how do we behave?
4. Present reality—where are we now?
5. Strategy—what is our action plan?
6. Performance agreement—how do we measure success?
7. Role definition—who is going to do what by when?

I have worked with many leaders who cannot answer these questions with certainty and wonder why people are not excited and engaged in their mission. If you and your core team cannot answer these seven questions without hesitation, do not expect the answers from your frontline people.

"The achievements of an organization are the results of the combined effort of every team member. Individual commitment to the mission that is what makes a team work, a company work, a society work, and civilization work." – Vince Lombardi

It's amazing to me how hard most leaders and their teams work but cannot answer these questions. Think how much more effective and efficient your team could be by simply knowing the answers. The energy level rises, the focus is sharper and positive results substantially greater.

You will never know where your team is mentally and emotionally unless you ask them these seven questions. Why do you continue leading a team without their hearts and minds in the game?

"If you don't know where you're going any road will get you there" —Lewis Carroll.

It's not enough for you to know—your team must know or it's like running a 100-yard dash with a safe on your back.

"Whether you turn to the right or to the left, your ears will hear a voice behind you, saying, this is the way walk in it." Isaiah 30:21

Day 29
Coaching Your Team to Victory!

Seminars and workshops are one-time events providing a lot of good information by very knowledgeable and professional presenters, bosses tell people what to do with that information, managers try to get people to work together around that information, but great team leaders coach their team to victory based on strong relationships over the best information.

Coaching is a journey—not an event. The coaching journey consists of five phases. Coaching leaders move through these five phases accomplishing the critical outcomes in each phase.

1. **RELATE:** You must establish a strong coaching relationship and agree on the agenda. Coaching at its core is about trust, connection, support and understanding, none of which is required by bosses or seminar presenters. Do not be tempted to skip the relationship building and move too soon to the core of the agenda—it seldom works well.

2. **REFLECT:** Identify and explore key issues. When you get lost in a mall, you go to the Directory sign and look for the "You are here" red dot. You cannot make effective and significant progress until there is agreement on current reality. Every journey must have a beginning and ending point of reference, if not, do not start the journey, it is called going from one unknown to another unknown—never a happy ending.

3. **REFOCUS:** Determine priorities and make a plan of action. The focus now shifts to vision, values and goals. Identify actions that make the greatest immediate impact and create the best ROI—return on investment. Address the questions of who, what, when, why and how, if not written, they do not exist.

4. **RESOURCES:** Provide support, encouragement and inspiration as foundational resources. Great leaders always look for ways to better leverage existing resources before asking for more of anything, and prove it. Many times more is not better, only a cover for poor performance. On the other hand, do not ask your team to more with less unless both agree, moving forward without it spells trouble.

5. **REVIEW:** Evaluate, celebrate and revise should not be options but a regular occurrence. Never underestimate the power of looking back over accomplishments and celebrating—just do not camp there. This phase maximizes learning and provides opportunities to make mid-course corrections. This phase provides both satisfaction for a job well done and much needed encouragement for the road ahead.

As a coaching leader you facilitate accountability, a steeper learning curve, greater challenges, celebrations for small and big wins, a sense of fulfillment, all in a healthy relationship using these five phases that leaves them clamoring for more.

"The apostles gathered together with Jesus (coach) and they reported to him all they had done and taught." —Mark 6:30

Day 30
Communication—the Art of Understanding and Being Understood

Communication is the cornerstone of any organization. Confusion has reigned since the serpent asked Eve in the Garden of Eden, *"Hath God not said...?"* Effective communication requires an absolute standard of truth that both parties understand and accept. The problem with communication is seldom over the facts—but the perception of those facts as truth.

Communicating effectively is not being a better public speaker or writing clearer memos. Great leadership communication is creating a compelling vision, a clear strategy, and an energizing set of values.

All leaders must routinely defend, clarify or announce actions in ways that acknowledge the multiple and often conflicting demands of their core leaders and influential stakeholders. Lacking strong communication skills, leaders in all organizations are ineffective at best or worse, irrelevant.

Communication clarity is leaderships' number one priority. It matters little how compelling your vision, how passionately you pursue it, or how deep your pockets; without understanding the hearts of your core leaders and they understanding yours, your best efforts are in vain.

Great leaders approach communication as a problem-solving skill—not a necessity to endure. What you say, when and where you say it, how you communicate vital information and reveal your leadership intent create a portrait of who you are and affects how your leadership is interpreted.

Dr. David Robinson

Great leaders learn to effectively communicate their vision, values, how resources are invested, managing events and leveraging time, spotting trends, and responding to crises in ways that benefit their organization, not their own personal interests.

Never let your passion to accomplish great things get in the way of understanding the hearts of your team. That always comes first, if not, disappointment sets in because it seems they never understand your heart's intent. Great communication always begins with listening first and then telling.

Day 31
Core Values – They Affect Everything

Upon the death of President Franklin Roosevelt near the end of World War II, Sam Rayburn, Speaker of the House, took V.P. Harry Truman aside and said, *"You're going to have a lot of people around you telling you what a great man you are, Harry. But you and I both know you ain't."* Truman ended up being a good president because his core values were fundamentally strong and guided his presidency.

Most organizations talk about core values, why you do things, what you stand for, and how they should govern our personal lives and work environment. But given a blank piece of paper and ask to write down 5-7 non-negotiable principles that dictate how you live your personal life or create the culture where you work most cannot do it.

After eight years of traveling over 250 days a year, working with hundreds of church and marketplace leaders, lack of commitment to the same core values creates most leadership and organizational problems.

Most leaders think their organization is values-based. They think everyone knows, supports, and lives them every day. This assumption by leaders creates most of their problems.

Do not think so; ask your team to list your team's core values by memory. If they cannot, I would bet the farm most of your leadership challenges are value-related issues.

Day 32
Developing Great Leadership Skills

Leading an organization, business, or church is not the same as managing the day-to-day affairs. Most great leaders can manage but know if they get lost in the weeds of the details, they forfeit the right and ability to influence the future.

I often tell leaders, you can manage the details or create the future, but you cannot do both, take your pick.

Here are seven skills leaders who create a compelling future develop

1. They cultivate a sense of compassion and responsibility for their team members before assigning their tasks.
2. They create and maintain an atmosphere that keeps the team, not only showing up, but also excited to be there.
3. They see things from more than one perspective, giving them greater flexibility in creating diverse teams, and not robots who cannot think for themselves.
4. They always challenge the status quo and never fear new opportunities or learning new skills.
5. They are bold—but not reckless in vision and strategic planning. They are meticulous—but not paralyzed by analysis.

6. They learn from mistakes, theirs and others. They know sometimes the best teachers are failures and poor bosses pose as leaders.

7. They are not drawn into public debates, but engage in respectful discussion and debate without being condescending and argumentative.

Day 33
Do You Have a Plan; Flip a Coin, or Just Hope?

Someone once said, "Responsibility is the great developer of men." I meet frustrated leaders all the time who say, "Where do I find mature, responsible, and capable leaders?" I quickly respond, "Even a blind squirrel finds an acorn once in a while, but most of the time they scurry around in the dark hoping to stumble on one." This describes the leadership development plan of most organizations, except for the great ones. You rarely find good leaders—you develop them.

Most organizations only look for a leader when they need one. That is one of the main reasons average organizations never develop greatness. The worst time to look for a leader is when you need one; the best time is when you do not. Great organizations are constantly looking for good leaders they can make great. When they find a potential candidate, even if they do not need them, they make a place for them on the team because good leaders are hard to find and great leaders are harder to keep.

Do you have a leadership development strategy (action plan), or do you start looking when there is a leadership vacancy? If you don't keep your leadership pipelines flowing most of the time you settle for second best when the need arises for a great leader.

Strategy is a military term meaning, it is about the whole and not the parts. Strategy has three hallmark features:

Long-term: you define what long-term means in your own context, but remember strategy is never about today. If it is short-term, it is more tactical than strategic.

It is important—never urgent: In operations, if not careful and intentional, the urgent overshadows the important. Strategic leadership is about thinking ahead, clearing the brush, leading the way, and make sure everyone is following.

Multi-components: There is always more than one element in strategy. It is made up of complementary components. Leadership selection, education, training and deployment must all work together.

Even great strategies have a limited shelf life. I often say, there is no such thing as a good strategic plan, but only a great strategic planning process. Strategic planning should not be a periodic event but a daily exercise. If you do not create a strategy for your own future, someone else will make you part of theirs.

If someone ask you today to share your vision in a couple of sentences and your plan to get there, what would you tell them.

Day 34
Does Setting Goals Really Matter?

When you set a goal, you tell yourself and everyone around you—this goal matters! You and everyone on the team must see the *"final frame"* (results) to stay energized and focused. Your action plan may not have all the answers before you take the first step but never let that prevent you from taking the first step. After you set a goal and commit to its success, the system God created in you helps you see it happen. Favor and resources start appearing that were not available previously.

Setting new goals always sets up a conflict between keeping things the way they are and creating something new. Holding two conflicting ideas in your mind at the same time is a skill all great leaders have mastered. The keepers of the status quo will always challenge those who want to create a future that is different from just another duplication of today. As a leader, you must make a choice or be frustrated with indecision. Your ability to handle this conflict determines your leadership effectiveness.

Great leaders inevitably resolve this conflict while poor leaders are continually frustrated with how things are and how they should be. Whenever your normal routines are challenged, your real leadership ability is revealed. It is at this point the importance of goals becomes evident. As you become dissatisfied with the old, you are energized and motivated by moving beyond the status quo and resolve the conflict by leading to the new. This is a way of life for all great leaders and only a dream for poor leaders.

Present reality keeps you either focused on your goals or bogged down in the same old routines. Great leaders understand the more you see your goals met and exceeded, the more energy and enthusiasm it creates to see new ones set and the cycle continue. This is the essence of leadership. The moment this cycle stops, you move from being a goal-setter—a leader, to being a problem-solver—a manager.

Every team needs both problem-solvers and goal-setters. Managers make today better because their goal is solving today's challenges—its chaos without them. However, someone on the leadership team must create the future or the value of whatever it is you do ceases to exist after one, or maybe two generations. Visionary leaders have an intense

desire, based on a clear vision, and a solid action plan. They stay focused on accomplishing the dream through setting goals and persuading the team to follow.

"We make our plans (set goals), but the Lord determines our steps (action plan)." Proverbs 16:9

Day 35
Does Setting Goals Really Matter? Part 2

Too many leaders kid themselves by ignoring present reality. Ninety percent are committed to a future that is idea oriented--but not goal driven. Leaders without goals are never guilty of missing the mark because they have no clear target. Great leaders are not sufficiently challenged until the risk of failure is clear and measured. The difference between winning and losing is commitment to action and finishing. Finishing with sustainable results is always your greatest challenge as a leader, but that never happens without legitimate goals and a commitment to complete the task.

Having hopes, dreams, good ideas and even strong desires are not the same as having specific and clearly defined goals. Here are seven steps to set and achieve worthwhile goals:

1. Write them down. Until goals are written—they remain only good ideas.
2. Goals must be clear and specific. They must answer the who, the what, the when, the why and the how questions. If yours do not—revise them. If you cannot measure your goals how can you track the progress, improve your efforts, and evaluate the results?
3. Set short-term goals. Without short-term wins you can get discouraged at best and worse, demoralized and abandon your long-term goals. Without long-term goals, you lose focus and never realize the ultimate dream.
4. Make sure your long-term goals stretch you but remain attainable. If you want to finish a marathon,

you do not run 26 miles the first day. Start small, stay at it, and never quit.

5. Plan for obstacles and setbacks, they come to everyone, especially those who are determined to set and achieve goals. It is better to fall short of your goal than to have no goal at all. Just like a good weld, we are stronger at the broken places. Tough times will make you more determined or cause you to quit.

6. Track your progress and reward your team. Consistent goal-setters measure the progress along the way while adjustments are possible, not just at the end when the results are final. Little victories keep you and your team energized and focused.

7. Affirm and visualize achieving your goals. If you cannot "see it"—you will never achieve it! Affirmation is confirming the truth of something verbally or in writing. Visualization is seeing the victory and achieving the goal before it happens.

It was said of Moses the great Israelite leader, "He endured seeing him who was invisible" Hebrews 11:27. Setting goals is one thing—achieving them quite another. Great leaders all have the ability to see the end before the beginning. Do not start the journey and ask people to follow you until you have a clear vision of its ending, the goals are set, and the commitment to finish is without question.

Day 36
Nothing Significant is Accomplished Without a Goal

"If a man proceeds confidently in the direction of his dreams and endeavors to live the life he has imagined, he will meet with success unexpected in common hours."
—Henry David Thoreau

I meet leaders all the time who have no clearly stated goals. Most are busy managing what is on their radar screen on any given day. Few are able to rise above the pressure of providing solutions while trying to focus on the next step critical to fulfilling their vision. The next step always has a goal or it is not the next step. Setting a goal is good, developing a plan is better, but executing the plan is best.

In 1953, Yale University surveyed the graduating class. Of the long list of questions asked, three related to setting goals. *"Do you set goals, do you write them down, and do you have a plan to reach them?"* Only three percent answered yes to the questions.

Twenty years later, they did a follow up study. As it turns out, the three percent who answered yes to setting goals with a plan to reach them reported they were more happily married, more successful in their carriers, better family life and better health. What was most astonishing was ninety-seven percent of the net worth of the class of '53 was in the hands of the three percent who started setting goals twenty years earlier.

When you have specific goals and accurate feedback about your progress, you open yourself up to a steady flow of opportunities that remains closed to those who have no clear goals and a plan to reach them.

Does setting goals really matter; will it make a significant difference in what you are doing? Yes! It did for the class of '53 at Yale. It mattered for President John Kennedy, whose leadership in 1969 sent a man to the moon and brought him home. That mission sparked a technology explosion that changed our world forever.

It did for the Apostle Paul when he said "*I have fought a good fight...finished my course...kept the faith*" in 2 Timothy 4:7. It did for Jesus when the Bible says of Him: "*Who for the prize set before Him, endured the shame of the cross*" Hebrews 12:2.

Setting goals and developing a plan to reach them is the essence of leadership. Managers execute the plan and make the numbers work. Leaders create the future by setting goals, managers are problem-solvers who figure out a way to reach them. Both are vital to your team's success.

Day 37
Effective Leadership is Built on Trust

In the comic strip Peanuts' Lucy was certainly a leader. She was also very good at sales. Most of the time she convinced the people around her that the advice she offered was worth the five pennies she charged. It seems she never had trouble getting the little round-headed kid to try one more time to kick the ball that she always pulled away at the last second.

Like Charlie Brown, most of want to trust the people around us. However, unlike Charlie Brown, few of us keep coming back to people who continually jerk the ball away when we try to kick it.

Great leaders establish trust before anything else, maintaining that trust is their highest priority. Trust is the glue that keeps every organization together and emotionally healthy. It does not matter if that effort is in the church world or the marketplace.

Without trust, personnel turnover is high, morale suffers and positive results are minimal.

Day 38
Leadership for the 21ˢᵗ Century

Until the later part of the 20th Century, Fortune 500 companies' and major ministry organizations' number one priority in searching for top leaders was the person's I.Q. and how productive they were. Those are still important, but the number one concern now is a person's E.Q., their emotional maturities. Their E.Q. determines how well they work with others and if they will make wise and mature decisions, especially during times of crisis and challenge.

E.Q., emotional maturity and awareness, is knowing who you are in Christ and who He is in you. How you respond to others, the situations you face, and the plans you have for the future is where all leaders must begin. It is this understanding of wholeness that determines your leadership effectiveness both now and in the future. Never has the church and its leaders faced a more challenging time in a world with such an uncertain future.

Leadership has changed dramatically both in the marketplace and the church. A whole new set of skills and attitudes are needed to have impact and influence. These skills and attitudes must be blended with a spiritual maturity and personal growth not demanded or even required up to this point in history. The Church must model Luke 2:52, the areas in which Jesus grew if she wants to compete on the world stage at a level that will fulfill the Great Commission to *"disciple nations."*

This leadership commitment must include a deep love for the Lord and a passion to do His will without compromise. Ministry leaders' skill sets must include an understanding and expertise in emerging technologies; an anticipation and grasp of new opportunities; mastering personal leadership capabilities; appreciating diversity; building partnerships and alliances; sharing leadership roles by creating a shared vision; knowing how to lead continual change and thinking globally.

To achieve this level of competency will require dedication, practice, patience and the zeal of the Apostle Paul, *"This one thing I do..."* It will also require a starting point. Every great effort not only has a beginning, but has an attitude; a mindset; a determination that things are going to change and it starts with the leader. That's what real leadership is about. It starts with your personal life; your local leadership opportunities; and your ability to see that you can make a difference...not only where you are, but globally as well.

You may not be the smartest leader, but you can be a mature leader. The Apostle Peter's final words include a warning for today's leaders during these very unsettling times around the globe.

"I am warning you ahead of time, dear friends. Be on guard so you will not be carried away by the errors of wicked people and lose your own secure footing. Rather, you must grow in the grace and knowledge of our Lord and Savior, Jesus Christ..." —2 Peter 3:17-18 NLT

Day 39
Authority—Use it, But First Make Sure You Have It

Jamie Dimon, CEO of JP Morgan Chase, since taking the reins of authority in 2005, shepherded the $2.3 trillion in assets through the global financial crisis and turned a $21.3 billion in 2012. He did it primarily through welding his authority—not building consensus. Authority was the only tool he could use effectively in the low-consensus cultural environment he inherited.

During the bank's integration with his previous bank, Bank One, convinced that salaries were out of control (the HR director was making more than $5 million), Dimon met with the executives to inform them they were vastly overpaid and cut their salaries 20%-50%. He drove a replacement of the firm's myriad IT systems with a single platform, threatening to make all the decisions himself if the IT staff did not reach any decisions within six weeks.

You may not understand all the dark secrets of the banking and investment industry, but regardless of the organization, a wise leader in a low-consensus culture would never agree to attempt significant changes without having all the authority needed to make those changes.

I'm not suggesting you bring your AK-47 to the office, however when organizational factions are in turmoil, can't agree what they want, and refuse to maintain a spirit of cooperation on how to reach some common goals—using your authority to make changes may be your only option.

There are more desirable change tools you can use, which I will share in future posts, but when all else fails and you should know that within the first 90 days, leaders must use the authority of their position to move towards change. There is a time to negotiate but don't use analyses, endless discussion and debate as a cover for lack of action. Do not allow a few dissenters to set the bar and pace of the changes that must invariably come.

Jim Ringo, five-time all pro center for the Green Bay Packers in the 60's, arrived to negotiate his contract with very successful head coach, Vince Lombardi, mistakenly bringing along his agent. Lombardi despised negotiating with players through their agents, feeling it weakened his ability to lead his team. Lombardi said, "I don't negotiate with agents", excused himself and left the room. Returning a few minutes later, he told Ringo, "You've been traded to Philadelphia." Lombardi not only had a title, he had authority to make change when it was best for the team.

Use authority rarely. Nevertheless, do not be afraid to use it, sometimes it is the only tool in your leadership bag that works.

Day 40
What Leaders Can and Cannot Do

Visionary leaders can only do what wide consensus on priorities allows. With new organizations it's the fiats of the founder that drives all the priorities and what gets done. Team members are promoted who fit within the established systems and have similar priorities and values—those who don't tend to leave.

In older organizations' only crisis, failures, and changing realities challenge the status quo and people are no longer certain about the future. Managers, that have now replaced the leaders, tend to double their efforts in what no longer works. Without leaders who know how to create the future, build a cooperative and motivated team, and a clear path to get there, the arguments begin but the battle is already lost.

In 1983, after a brilliant career at PepsiCo, John Scully was tapped to replace founder, Steve Jobs at Apple, but by the late 80's Scully knew Apple was in trouble for a variety of reasons but the employees were deeply entrenched in their culture and not motivated to change.

Scully tried reorganization, firings, control systems, financial incentives, vision statements, strategic planning and everything he knew worked at PepsiCo with no success. His team, not impressed, he lost his credibility and fired in 1993.

Apple's board hired Michael Spindler, head of their successful European operation. He tried to change the culture unsuccessfully and dismissed six months later. The board then chose Gil Amelio, turn-around specialist at National Semiconductor. He failed and was gone in 18 months.

Unable to recruit another top CEO, Apple's board in desperation, turned to their founder, Steve Jobs, as interim CEO. Jobs ceased trying to change the culture and instead encouraged the team to go back to designing innovative, high-end products such as the iMac and the iPod. Result, Apple now dominates the digital music industry.

The lesson for all leaders, if Scully would have understood and used the right tools to elicit cooperation behind the direction he knew Apple must go, Apple might have captured much of the business that ultimately went to Compaq, Dell and Microsoft. Scully would have lost the argument but saved his job and profits for Apple—off the chart.

One of the rarest leadership skills is the ability to understand which change tools work in which situations – and not waste time, energy, resources, and risk credibility using tools that will not. Ultimately, your long-term success as a leader is tied to this fundamental ability.

Day 41
Great Leaders Don't Need a Chicken

In 1958 Mobil Travel Service, now Forbes Travel Service launched its star rating system to rank hotels and restaurants in their quality of service. Millions of people worldwide now use their rating system when planning their travel. The more stars the better the service.

In an old wise tale, a farmer tells his hired hand to take a chicken and kill it where no one can see. In a few hours, the hired man returns with a live chicken. *"Why didn't you kill it?"* asks the farmer. *"Because everywhere I go the chicken sees!"* responded the hired man.

Great leaders don't need a chicken to make sure they operate with honesty and integrity. Telling the truth is honesty, telling it all the time is integrity. Every decision in life has a moral or ethical component. You should be able to explain that decision the same way to anyone who asks whether it is your spouse, core leadership team, stakeholders, the New York Times or Fox News.

America's youth are confused growing up in country where in the past 40 years at least two Presidents have been publicly shamed for lying. One lied about having nothing to do with hiring men to break into his opposition's headquarters and steal election strategies during a very tough political campaign. The second had an affair with a young White House intern then promptly denied it for weeks. His eventual explanation gave an entirely new meaning for lying when he said, "It all depends on what the meaning of is—is."

Thank God, for men like James Burke, former CEO of Johnson & Johnson, who made a very difficult decision in

1982 to destroy millions of dollars of product after seven people died in Chicago taking Tylenol laced with cyanide. On the other hand, Paul Galvin, former CEO of Motorola whose credo was, "Tell the truth the first time, because it's the right thing to do and they will find out anyway."

Honesty and integrity are not options for great leaders and successful organizations, but the bedrock for every act they perform and every decision they make. In the long-term, there is no fundamental tradeoff between honesty and integrity and financial success--just the opposite. Regardless of your field of leadership, cheating, however minor, may bring short-term gains but the long-term price is just not worth it!

Psalms 7:8 says, *"Judge me, O Lord, according to my...integrity."*

Day 42
Kindness Does Not mean you're a Wimp

The rapid growth of Starbucks is well known. What is not so well known is that founder; Steve Schultz based his business model on kindness and compassion. He learned this philosophy as a working-class youth in Brooklyn whose father never experienced anything like the Golden Rule. Schultz's father had a number of blue-collar jobs at which he rarely received benefits and even rarer felt like a valued team member.

Growing up in the 60's I learned quickly that the prevailing business model was *"command and control."* This style of leadership, better named management, assumed that people are naturally lazy and need frequent reprimands or threats to get maximum effort. Kindness and compassion were considered an invitation to slack off and let others do the heavy lifting.

Showing compassion and kindness does not just feel better--it also builds confidence, adds to the bottom line, creates a healthy work environment, increases loyalty and productivity. In your push to achieve team goals do not overlook individual emotional needs—no matter tough they look on the outside or how harsh their tone. Most of the time it is a cover for past fears, failures and hurts.

Holding the team to high standards and showing people you really care are not mutually exclusive. My experience over 47 years of leadership experience shows just the opposite. Great leaders model kindness and compassion every day in successful organizations—thus the low staff turnover.

The productive and supportive tone of every great place to work is set in the front office and shows on the front lines— you can rely on it. The opposite tone, if not corrected, shows up when you least desire it—you can take it to the bank.

Herb Kelleher, former CEO of southwest Airlines, was perhaps America's most passionate corporate leader for the cause of love in the workplace. Without apology he said, *"We'd rather have a company run by love than by fear."* Southwest flies out of Dallas' Love Field, its stock exchange symbol are *"Luv,"* the company communication is called Luv Live, and its 20th Anniversary slogan was *"Twenty Years of Loving You."* They just happen to be one of America's most profitable airlines.

Kindness and compassion are signs of strength, not weakness. *"Love has no fear because mature love expels all fear. If we are afraid it's because we fear being judged"* 1 John 4:18.

Day 43
Creating a Culture of Justice and Fairness

"Organizations that are willing to share, withhold in order to further the growth, willing to try to get a better atmosphere through a demonstration of fairness and cooperation, those will win in the end." —E.O. Wilson, two-time Pulitzer Prize winner.

Justice means giving and receiving what a person deserves. Fairness is the ability to make judgments that are not overly general but that are concrete and specific to a particular situation. Determining what is just and fair is one of leaderships' greatest challenges on a daily basis. When there is only piece of pie left and two people want it, let one make the cut and the other choose the first piece—oh if life were only that simple!

Its one thing for a leader to pursue just policies and actions from the beginning, but often a leader must have the courage to confront and correct injustices especially those created by someone else. It is not enough to pursue justice and fairness, great leaders reverse injustices and issue appropriate rewards quickly.

It is very difficult keeping team members energized and loyal if they feel others are taking advantage, regardless if that person is at the top or in the cubicle next door. If people perceive they are being treated unfairly, they will eventually stop performing or they will start acting like those they perceive are being favored.

Five Star Leaders operate on principles of fairness because they know it inspires better performance, loyalty and retention. Honesty and integrity is primarily dealing with individuals—justice and fairness is about team dynamics. Work environments' without justice and fairness are not a fun place to go every day. Your job as a leader is to change that. If you do not expect many unhappy campers and watch as productivity drops. You cannot make everyone happy and at some point those who refuse to be team players must be let go. No matter how much you do for them, it is never just for fair.

No effective and productive organization, profit or nonprofit, is a true democracy. When an organization or even entry-level teams have no clear and respected leader, you have chaos. Multiple leaders are a myth; unfair and unjust leaders have usually abused those clamoring for it. But leaders who do not lead with a basic sense of justice and fairness soon lose the trust and loyalty of their followers. Great leaders never use their position or power to make and enforce arbitrary decisions for their own good or personal ambitions.

"Blessed are those who maintain justice, who constantly do what is right." —Psalms 106:3

Day 44
Purpose—the Power to Create or Remake

In his book *The Purpose Driven Life,* Rick Warren asked the question, *"What on Earth am I here for?"* What is the purpose for all the roles you play is one of life's fundamental questions. Most people work harder on the why and how questions when they should be asking—what is the purpose?

The ability to create a clear, compelling purpose and stay focused is often the difference between winning and losing, regardless of the endeavor. This ability, or lack of it, separates average leaders from the great ones.

The former Steve Jobs, when CEO of Apple, challenged John Scully to leave PepsiCo and join his startup company that lacked resources and name recognition. Jobs could not offer him more money or security, but instead offered him purpose, the chance to change the way the world communicates, learns and exchanges information--instead of making sugar water.

When a leader is dedicated to a purpose, the power to create something new or recreate something and make it better, the energy increases and the dedication is stronger. When all the stakeholders see that the commitment to fulfill the *purpose* is unwavering, great things happen. The mission connected to your purpose must be bigger than you are and outlive your lifetime or it is not big enough. No leader ever unified the efforts of people, raised substantial resources, and successfully achieved the impossible without an unwavering sense of purpose.

Great leaders' capabilities are more than charismatic personalities, communication styles, and mastering the art of persuasion, useless without understanding your purpose. In successful organizations, the purpose continues long after leadership changes. Your greatness as a leader is determined after you are gone—what can they do without you and is the purpose intact?

Hurdles, obstacles, and crisis test every leader's best efforts. In fact, it is these very challenges that create your purpose. There is no autopilot or default position for purpose. You cannot take your eye off your purpose for long without it derailing your entire effort. Tough times are the breakfast of champion leaders—they thrive on them.

Adversity quickly stops a weak or inexperienced leader without purpose, but it only fans the flames of great leaders who do not know the meaning of cannot or quit. It must be more than talk; you must do everything on purpose if you want to be a Five Star Leader.

"But this one thing I do; forgetting what is behind and straining toward what is ahead, I press toward the goal (purpose)." —Philippians 3:12-14

Day 45
You don't Manage People...you Correct their Performance

"A leader who does not correct people is squandering a precious resource. I think one of the things forget is that people look to us to tell them the truth in terms of how they are doing." —Charles Wang, former CEO of Computer Associates and present owner of the New York Islanders professional hockey team.

People don't want to be managed but they do want you to help them perform their job better.

There at least three ways you can help your team improve their performance. First, help them set ambitious yet realistic goals. Second, be a constant source of encouragement. Be a *"Hope Dealer"* and their Number One fan. No one ever overdosed on encouragement. Third, constantly communicate the agreed upon expectations before, during, and after their performance.

Consequences are a fact. Every decision comes with its own consequences positive or negative, none escapes. If there is no consequence for poor behavior, expect no change or improvement. Great leadership is about knowing when to issue the consequence, do they major surgery or just a Band-Aid? If there is no reward for outstanding performance, expect productivity to slow back down to average. Everyone must be held accountable for his or her performance. Great leaders teach people how to hold themselves accountable and reward them appropriately.

Learn to use rewards appropriately. At Custom Research, a marketing company with about 100 employees, owners Jeff and Judy Pope took a large chuck of their profits to reward the entire staff when the won the coveted Baldridge Award in 1996. They took everyone to London for five days all expenses paid. Some may say it was extravagant and overkill for a small company. Jeff Pope said, *"Not at all, it was money well spent. If you share the pie it gets larger."*

Five-Star Leaders are forgiving of honest mistakes made in the pursuit of performance goals. They know how to separate people from *"who"* they are from their performance. A bad performance does not make you a bad person. If you want a person's performance to improve, support them as a person and help them, correct their own actions—never reverse the process.

"He who heeds discipline shows the way of life...but whoever ignores correction leads others astray." —Proverbs 12:1

Day 46
Leading Teams or Managing Silos?

The term "silo," coined in the late 80 refers to internal competition leading to strife between individuals and departments within an organization. Silo builders are concerned only with what affects him or her. One of the frequent problems I deal with is leaders who want to build a team out people acting like silos. They babysit individuals whose main concern is, not the team's mission but their own agenda and comfort level.

Silo behavior is withholding information and knowledge and not sharing openly and honestly. Team members have very little meaningful dialogue with each other, seldom share resources, and rarely offer to help others unless asked directly and then only grudgingly. Individuals and departments focus only on achieving their goals at the expense of others, sometimes even the detriment of the entire organization. Yes, silo builders are team players as long as you play on their team.

There are three primary reasons why people are silo builders. First, they fear that if a mistake occurs, they get the blame; they always want the credit but never the blame. Second, the desire to create a *"comfort zone"* that provides order, consistency and familiarity—a place to hide. Third, they feel the need to create informal rules--a zone of relative predictability. These rules soon become an irrational line-in-the-sand, *"that's the way I (never we) do things around here."*

Silos, regard less if it's a business, church, or Ladies Tea Club, are a drain productively, lead to redundancies, poor communication and most of all, a lack of trust. When internal conflict and competition develops, an unhealthy environment takes over and positive results diminish. Mess with a silo builder and watch how soon the protection of turf begins in earnest, if not corrected they do a lot of damage to the entire farm. Great leaders do not allow that to happen, they say— join the team or take your silo to another farm.

The average American spends one third of their life getting ready to work, traveling to and from work, and working. If you start at age 21 and retire at 65, you invest well over 100,000 hours. You can spend it building your own silo or be a team player and leverage your personal efforts far beyond what you could ever accomplish alone.

"One can put a thousand to flight and two can chase ten thousand." Deuteronomy 32:30

Day 47
Please Hand me the Tomato Soup—a Lesson in Courage

I remember the story about a little girl who was afraid of the dark. She lived in an old farmhouse where they kept food in a pantry that to her was dark and intimidating. Her mother, preparing dinner, asks her to get a can of tomato soup out of the pantry. She peered behind the curtain leading to the pantry that had no light or windows, being scared she ran back to her mother empty handed.

"Where's the soup?" asked her mother. The little girl, shaking, replied, *"Its dark in there, I'm afraid."* Three times her mother sent her back and she went as far as the curtain and ran back without the soup. Finally her mother said, *"Don't be afraid of the dark, Jesus is in the dark, he'll protect you."* Slowly the little girl returned to the pantry curtain, pulled it back and said, *"Jesus, if you're in there would you please hand me a can of tomato soup?"*

It's a funny story and while most people outgrow their fear of the dark as a child, most adults still lack the courage to face the unknown or uncertainty. Jack Welch, one of the 20th Century's top corporate leaders as CEO of General Electric, spent most of his time developing leaders. He constantly drilled the potential senior leaders and managers on what separates great leaders from the average is the *"courage"* to make the tough calls decisively, with fairness and absolute integrity, especially *"in the dark"*—when the outcome is uncertain.

Courage will permeate and transform everything you do; it is this crucial seasoning in your leadership skill mix God blesses. Take away courage from a leader and you are left with a functionary who can only enforce the manual. Rules and regulations are needed to keep order but they are not the tools of leaders who create the future—but managers who respond to today's challenges. There are no manuals for the future. You need guts to enforce the rulebook but you need courage to create the future.

Someone once said, *"Courage is fear that has said its prayers."* Leaders who are brutally honest about the risks inspire people and obstacles but go for it anyway. Adversity energizes and motivates courageous leaders, but quickly quenches the fire in leaders without courage.

There is a fine line between faith and fanaticism and only the courageous leaders walk that line, the rest follow in the shadows—a safer place. When you are hitting short-term difficulties, remember, your long-term goals create the courage to go on. Seldom does life *"hand you the tomato soup"*—you have to go into the unknown and get it—that takes courage.

"If you falter in times of trouble, how small is your strength." —Proverbs 24:10

Day 48
Winning the Argument but Losing the Battle

The best way to win an argument is never have one. No one "wins" an argument. Even if you win, you lose. You may lose a job, a friend, a marriage, something is lost in every argument. Arguments are usually the result of inflated egos and a mind of granite—the price of victory is seldom worth the emotional, physical and many times the financial costs.

Leaders who want to move their organization in a new direction must first understand the degree to which the team already agrees on two dimensions—what everyone wants personally out of being on the team and cause and effect, or how to achieve what they want in the future. Ignore those two issues and expect resistance to the changes you are proposing no matter how great you think they can help.

What tools you use in bringing change depends on where the team is located on the *"agreement continuum"* —what point between high agreement and low agreement, what the team wants now, in the future and how to get there. Clear consensus on both determines their willingness to change or how strong the resistance, do not make assumptions—let there be no doubts before introducing the change process.

Team members generally satisfied with the way things are and strongly agree on how to maintain the status quo are always the last to change—if ever. Great leaders know which tool to use, when, and how to use it in making major changes. Never forget, any change is major to someone, especially the person who has the most to lose when the change comes.

The change tools that foster and inspire change at one end of the consensus continuum will not work at the other end. There is no *"best"* position on the agreement continuum for change, it's just your present reality and where you must start. However, a particular change tool works better than the others do at that point.

"Leadership is getting people to do what you want them to do, how you want them to do it, when you want them to it; because they want to do it."—General Dwight Eisenhower

Day 49
Treat Everyone Fairly—but not the Same

Phil Jackson, the highly regarded professional basketball coach of the Chicago Bulls and Los Angeles Lakers, won more championships than any coach in the history of professional sports did. A preacher's kid from North Dakota, he used one foundational principle common to all great leaders, he led by inspiring and not belittling his players. He inspired multi-million dollar star athletes, driven by out-of-control egos, to change from being a star to being team players, producing eleven championships.

What was his secret? How was he able to win the argument and the battle? Jackson understood the fundamentals of basketball, being an average player at best, but his greatest asset was winning the argument for change in the minds of his players. He knew you must treat everyone fairly but seldom do you treat two the same way. Producing team-minded champions out of super-stars is no different from taking people with a *"loser"* mentality and making them winners—you just start at the opposite end; both groups must learn to pull together.

The first step in making significant changes is assessing the present level of agreement, between team members, departments, divisions or any separate entities that must work together. Do not let anyone put a positive spin on where that level is, or whether it exists at all—brutal honesty is always the starting point. If you do not start there, eventually the truth will surface anyway—no *"Texas hold'em"* allowed.

If you cannot agree on what already exists, it's even harder to agree on what you want. Do not rush the conversation or limit the participation in the discussion that must include; individual values, priorities, which tradeoffs everyone is willing to make, and a dozen other topics that are sure to come up.

Second, is the extent to which people agree on cause and effect—which actions best lead to the desired results. You must agree on cause and effect before taking any action, if not, you may win the argument but you will lose the battle. If you move change too fast, I guarantee some will come kicking, screaming, and team morale tanks.

It's better to delay action and deal with people's lack of understanding or just plain obstinacy. If they refuse to come around offer them some options for remaining on the team or release them if all else fails. Great leaders know that some good people who helped pull the wagon to where it is are no longer valuable to the team in pulling it further because they are unable or refuse to make the critical changes. If you do not release them, you will lose the battle.

"After David served his own generation well, he fell asleep..." —Acts 13:36

Day 50
When Communication Goes Bad

On January 13, 1982, Air Florida Flight 90 was due to travel from Washington National Airport in Virginia to Hollywood International Airport in Fort Lauderdale.

Conditions were snowy, and the first officer noticed that something was wrong with the plane's instruments and that it was not capable of getting airborne because of being de-iced improperly. However, his attempts to communicate this were brushed off by the captain, who ordered the take-off to continue.

The plane crashed into the 14th Street Bridge, killing 78 people, including four motorists. Later, reports showed that there was sufficient space for the aircraft's take-off to be aborted—if only the flight crew had been communicating better.

Leaders who cannot communicate clearly and simply should forfeit their right to lead. The best plans, ideas and directives are useless unless communicated well. Today's electronic communication overload has made face-to-face communication even more critical. Most people receive dozens of emails and texts from team members in the next cubicle. Long distance communication means down the hall.

The seven principles of good communication have not changed since people began talking to each other. Good communication is clear, concise, concrete, correct, coherent, complete, and courteous. Make sure every email, conference call, meeting, and report meets that standard or do not release it until it does.

Great communication begins with great listening—not speaking. All great leaders listen well. They share information openly and widely; they know people are going to find out any way and usually from a less desirable source. Five-Star leaders leverage the power of individual and group communication.

By engaging in open and honest communication you gain increased loyalty from both inside and outside customers, you stimulate the flow of new ideas, and create a healthy, productive and non-threating work environment. The further away from the *"inner sanctum"* the more accurate and adequate information is needed. Most employee frustration would evaporate if they just had the honest information.

Sixty-nine people on Air Florida flight 90 and four passengers on the 14th Street Bridge would be alive today if the pilot had listened to his team. How many stars would you give the pilot that day? All leaders make judgment errors but poor communication should not be one.

Day 51
Know What Leadership Tool to Use and When

The primary task of a leader is creating the future and building a core team of managing leaders who know how to build a front line team of passionate, dedicated and cooperative team members that embrace the changes critical for that future.

In 1999, Proctor and Gamble's new CEO, Durk Jager, highly regarded by many announced Organization 2005, a restructuring program promising to bring sweeping changes to P&G's culture. However, not everyone at P&G agreed those sweeping changes were needed or the way to achieve its goal of reducing investments in its core product line in order to create new products.

The organization rebelled and forced Jager to resign just 17 months after he assumed leadership, He won the initial argument but lost the war. The root cause of his failure was his inability to create a spirit of cooperation across the board before implementing his sweeping changes. This highly touted, super CEO made a rookie mistake and paid for with his job.

To achieve broad cooperation, first commandment of great leadership, require team leaders have a variety of tools in their leadership bag and know which tool to use—when and where. The effectiveness of the tool depends a lot on the organization's culture, experience and maturity of the leader, and clarity about present reality on multiple levels.

You can use a variety of sticks and carrots to encourage cooperative changes, but your success in getting positive and sustainable change is determined by your ability to read people, their perception of reality, and the circumstances in which you are attempting change.

Making changes is like directing an orchestra, the more talented and motivated the musicians, the harder it is to keep them playing together and producing a final product that everyone enjoys. Even the best CEO's have stumbled in their attempts to get people to *"see the big picture"* before the vision becomes a reality.

Do not let your ego cause you to win the argument but lose your leadership ability to influence the outcome of the war. You cannot win if you are no longer in the game. Sometimes the need to be right keeps us from growing. Because you are the top banana on the flow chart does not mean you know everything, it should mean you have the ability to form a team that together can find the answer to any challenge.

When I stepped out of my little space I called rightness and looked around at the vastness and complexity of the universe and said, *"Wow, just maybe I could be wrong,"* was when my real maturing as a leader began. It was very liberating not to have to know everything!

Day 52
Don't Judge Accuracy by Battles Won

Winning an argument doesn't make you right or the points of your defense true. Too often disagreements turn from being a search for the truth into a battle for being "right." We all know, but hard for many to accept, you can win an argument and still be wrong. Don't judge the accuracy of your beliefs by how many battles they survive.

Arguments and debates can guide us to the truth if everyone comes to the table with the same degree of openness, sets their biases aside and puts their egos in their back pockets. Exchanging ideas, exposure to criticism, considering new perspectives are all excellent ways to challenge our personal truth.

As a leader, you may not be as persuasive, as articulate, and as quick on your feet as others, but that is no excuse for not having all the information you need and fully prepared to defend your position. When you are trying to implement change, it's not about how loud or long you argue it's about being fully persuaded of the change tools you are using, but without blinders.

In addition to your positional authority (power tools), there are three other tools leaders can use to generate a cooperative team culture—leadership tools, culture tools, and management tools.

If your team wants the same thing but disagrees on how to achieve it, leadership tools such as inspiration, role modeling and personal attention can achieve it. If the team agrees on cause and effect but little on what they want, you can use management tools such as training, financial incentives, strategic planning, and measurement systems.

If your team is stuck in the status quo—they agree on what they want today and how to get it, you must adjust the corporate culture to make significant changes—the most difficult of the four tools to implement. Changing organizational culture is all about values, rituals, tradition and *"the way it's always been"*—extremely difficult.

Organizations with strong cultures (value systems) instinctively prioritize similar options, and their common view of how "their" world works means that very little debate is needed about the best way to achieve their priorities and goals. These kinds of organizations are almost self-managing, but this strength makes them also highly resistant to change.

"Today's kids are not ADD, they're EOE: Engage Me or Enrage Me." Kip Leland in the book, **"Don't Bother Me Mom—I'm Learning."**

Sometimes we are trying to win arguments for change when we do not have our teams attention must less their engagement. In your passion to make changes, you can only go as fast as the slowest person on the team is willing—think otherwise and trouble begins.

Day 53
How to Avoid being Overworked and Overwhelmed

Poor leaders find their selves running out of time while their direct reports lack motivation and running out of productive work. Great leadership is not about personal production but team production.

Delegation is one of leaderships most important strengths and doing it well a must for effectives and significant success. Great leaders spend less time "doing" and the bulk of their time planning, organizing resources, and coaching their team.

There is a major difference between delegating and deferring. Delegating means, you still own some of the responsibility for the results. Deferring means you give it away and no longer have any responsibility. Great leaders use both and know when and how to use them.

Some warning signs you need to improve your delegating skills

- Your in-box is always full with work only you can do.
- Delegated assignments are often incomplete and deadlines missed.
- Direct reports feel they lack authority, resources, and empowerment.
- You constantly second guess team members' decisions.
- Team morale is low, turnover rates rising, and people lack motivation.

- You frequently intervene in work you previously assigned.
- Team members feel unprepared and not taking full responsibility.

Six tips for delegating effectively

1. Recognize and affirm the capabilities of your team for their assignments.
2. Focus on results—not how tasks should be accomplished.
3. Use delegation to develop the skills of your team members and position them for advancement.
4. Always delegate to the lowest level possible.
5. Explain assignments clearly and provide necessary resources.
6. Provide consistent feedback, support during tough times, and celebrate all wins.

Overworked and overwhelmed leaders are leaders who failed to learn how to delegate effectively.   As a result, your best people leave you because they are bored, you hold back the development of your good people, and your average workers are burned up or burned out because of trying to do it all.

Day 54
Does a Group indicate a Team?

Sam Walton, founder of Walmart, favorite mantra was *"Our people make the difference."* This message is posted on the back of the company's trucks and the walls of its warehouses. Managers who have been disciplined or fired for abusing or ignoring people can't say they didn't see the *"writing on the wall."*

Larry Bossidy, former CEO of Allied Signal, realizes the importance of every team member: *"You've got to make sure everyone understands how important they are to the team. As a leader, you need people more than they need you."* If you don't believe it, ask the former coach of any professional sports team or the dismissed CEO of any major organization.

Teams are made of stones that come in all shapes and sizes and very unpredictable—not production bricks that are uniform and predictable. A journeyman bricklayer can lay a good wall with bricks, but it takes a master mason to build a stonewall—no two being the same.

Building a team with a group of people dedicated to the same mission and outcome is different than providing a work opportunity for a group of people who show up at the same place every day. One provides a job in exchange for a paycheck, while the other provides an opportunity to make a significant difference by leveraging their personal efforts with that of their team.

Great team leaders do 7 things well

1. Create a clear and compelling vision.
2. Set challenging but reasonable standards.

3. Create short-term direction and long-term focus.
4. Fire passion, creativity and innovation.
5. Generate buy-in and synergy.
6. Develop their team's full potential and sense of empowerment.
7. Set and accomplish goals.

A carefully selected team with complementary skills and strengths, dedicated to the team, outperforms a collection of talented individuals all competing to be the "star."

"As iron sharpens iron, so one man sharpens another." Proverbs 27:17

Day 55
Developing Leaders vs. Gathering Followers

According to the American Society of Training and Development, U.S. companies and organizations, both profit and nonprofit, spend more than $170 Billion annually on leadership-based curriculum and training. Training is the number one reason leadership development fails.

You don't train leaders—you develop leaders. You train animals that have very little, if any, reasoning power. When you treat your team, especially future leaders, like animals and try to train them rather than individual independent thinkers - leadership development grinds to a halt.

Training presumes the need for indoctrination on systems, processes and techniques, assuming all of that are *"doing things the right way."* All valuable but have little to do with leadership development. When seminar presenters refer to something as *"best practices,"* rest assured it's probably not.

Training involves best practices, but leadership development focuses on next practices. Training workshops are often by the book, one dimensional, one directional; one size fits all, an authoritarian process that imposes static and outdated information. An untested, inexperienced professional presenter in a monologue who rarely goes off script presents most of it. Scripts contain good information but battle-tested veterans are your best bet for developing future leaders.

Worst of all this *"training"* usually occurs in a vacuum driven by someone else's experience - not the needs of future leaders. You cannot develop leaders in classrooms, seminars and workshops. Those venues are for dispensing information and testing to see if you understand the generic information. Leaders are developed under live fire. Leaders need the information but if you want to know if they really understand it, see how they do when the bullets are flying.

There is an old parable that says, *"Give a man a fish and he eats for a day, teach him how to fish and he eats for a lifetime."* It is true for leadership. Develop a leader for a generation and that generation thrives. Develop leaders in every generation, not just followers, and that organization thrives for succeeding generations.

Great leaders have the ability to attract people—but a greater ability to develop future leaders, renew the passion for the vision and consistently find new leaders to execute the mission. Never let your desire to *"grow" your organization distract* you from your main purpose—developing new leaders that create the way forward. Sustainable growth always outlasts explosive growth.

"Praised be the Lord, who has allowed me to see a successor on my throne today." —1 Kings 1:47

Day 56
5 Things Great Leaders Never Compromise

Compromise, is it a leadership strength or weakness? According to Dictionary.com, the word compromise means, "A settlement of differences by mutual concessions; an agreement reached by adjustment of conflicting or opposing claims and principles by reciprocal modification of demands."

In Steven Covey's book, *The Third Alternative*, Covey contrasts compromise and synergy. He illustrates Compromise as -1+1 = 1.5 and Synergy as -1+1 = 3. Covey adds, *"Do you catch yourself agreeing to compromise simply because you don't want to invest the time and effort to create synergy, or because the other person won't pursue synergy with you?"*

Leaders must lead and sometimes the only way of moving forward within the available time constraints is compromise—but never at the expense of essential principles, trust, and integrity. Compromise is a management tool used often, but rarely used by leaders. Great leaders never leave problems unresolved or team members frustrated by kicking the can down the road through compromise.

Here are five things great leaders never compromise

1. Maintaining the balance between pursuing the vision with passion, developing their core leader's fullest potential, and managing the team's mission responsibly.

2. Developing a saturation communication and wise decision-making culture through accurate, adequate and shared information; coupled with open, honest, and collaborative conversations.

3. Staying engaged with their team; mentally, emotionally, and spiritually while remaining focused on enlarging the team's leadership capacity and capability.

4. Mobilizing and enlarging the team's vision through a resonant, shared, and resourced purpose.

5. They model and keep the team's shared value system-- the motivation and inspiration for creating a productive working and serving environment.

Compromise is neither strength nor weakness, but a tool great leader's only use until they find a way to create a "win-win" solution, no one loses. In a compromise, everyone loses something and the best decisions are seldom made.

Day 57
Conflict—Tolerate it or Resolve it

"There are three ways of dealing with differences: domination, compromise and integration. By domination only one side gets what it wants; by compromise neither side gets what it wants; by integration both find a way to get what they wish."—Mary Parker Follett

Resolving conflicts requires all parties come together voluntarily, agree on the issues, and work cooperatively to resolve the differences. Most of the time the process works best with a trained and mature facilitator.

The process should, reflect your organization's values, show respect for every individual, be modeled by core leaders, and require full participation in a spirit of openness, honesty and emotional maturity.

The facilitator should gather the facts, identify key issues without making accusations, and encourage both sides to focus on the critical issues - not who did what, why, when, and assigning blame.

Each party should feel empowered to speak their mind, feel they have been heard, and understand they are a part of the solution. Therefore, should each party listen, respect, and understand everyone else's point of view, even if they disagree, they actively pursue a positive win-win decision.

This process only works if all team members

1. Accept differences as a way of life without disconnecting from the resolution process.

2. Everyone improves their persuasion skills.
3. Build confidence in recognizing win-win solutions.
4. Admit to and improve your own level of emotional maturity.
5. Find mutual points of agreement with those you differ.
6. Improve your listening skills.
7. Learn to disagree and not damage or lose friendships.

Great leaders find the good in everyone, they know even their enemies keep them focused on their goals.

"Ten percent of conflict is due to difference of opinion and ninety percent is due to the wrong tone of voice."
—*Vea* Mariz

Day 58
Seven Ways to Measure Your Values

How can you be sure your organization practices what you preach about your values? No matter how much you *"preach"* about the products or services you provide if you don't model quality values all your preaching is in vain and it's not long before it shows in your products or services.

Seven ways you can insure your actions match your articulation

1. Consistently gather reliable information broadly and deeply from all stakeholders, especially those closest to the front lines. Plumb the depths of their priorities, concerns, goals and problems. It's the values lived on the front lines that count--not the values on the wall of the CEO's office.

2. Create new values or adjust existing values based on new information. Your personal values may never change but some of the best organizational value statements are continuously evaluated, challenged, debated, and revised.

3. Promote your values often and by every means possible. Model them consistently at every level. If not, change your behavior to reflect your values, or change your values to match your behavior. Lack of passion and commitment reigns in many organizations because leaders cannot get this figured out.

4. Highlight how your values play a major role in your success. How they preserve integrity in unexpected and critical events or times of crisis. How you turn

down, not only questionable opportunities, but also legitimate opportunities because they conflict with your values.

5. Create and implement monitoring systems that verify how well your values are integrated and support your operational culture on a daily basis—not just occasionally. If your values do not guide your passions and actions rest assured someone else's will.

6. Teach your core leaders and managers at every level to acknowledge your organization's values in every decision until they are a way of life for all team members. Promotion and rewards should be as much about living the values as it is about the numbers.

7. Celebrate and reward, not only the top producers, but also everyone who reflects and sets the pace in modeling your core values. If you don't it's not long and it's a battle for numbers in a very unhealthy work environment.

Remember, values are not the same as aspirations. You can measure values—but not aspirations.

Day 59
Five Things to Look For in Future Leaders

1. The usual characteristics—competence, intelligence, character, moral courage, firmness with kindness, ability to inspire and loyalty.
2. They stand by their convictions, argue their position, but execute the teams' best decision as if it were their own.
3. They have imagination, creativity and the ability to anticipate problems and solutions.
4. They have constant awareness of their relationship with God, their team leader, their team members and the team's common vision.
5. They know the difference between managing and leading. They know great management is getting 100% of the teams' capabilities, but great leadership is seeking higher ground, setting high but achievable standards and goals with maximum effort.

Future leaders' resumes are usually thin but make sure of these five qualities before you appoint because you may have to dis-appoint.

Day 60
Do you have the right People on Your Core Team?

Here are five ways that indicate if you have the right people, doing the right thing, doing it in the right place and doing it at the right:

1. They are committed to God, their family, their leader, the vision and the action plan—in that order. If they do not have their personal core values in order, they will not prioritize yours correctly.

2. Team goals are always superior to any personal ambition; they energize and focus their efforts and those of their team members.

3. They develop leaders, not just followers, and credit the Team for all the wins. If they have leadership potential, recruiting and developing future leaders is a passion—not an afterthought.

4. On their team, they inspire the "A's" to maximum potential, they nurture the "B's" to competence and release the "C's" (vision drainers) before too much damage takes place. They recruit well but not afraid to release non-productive team members—sooner rather than later.

5. They are low maintenance, self-starters, finish consistently and loyalty is unquestionable. If you have team members who do just the opposite, why are they still on your team?

Day 61
Getting the Best from those you Lead

"The simple things, the true things, the silent men who do things" is a line from Jack London's book, *The Call of the Wild*. Great leaders silently pursue the vision with a sense of responsibility to finish with excellence. They learn early that getting the best efforts from those you lead is the top priority in the process. Reaching the goal is a by-product of great leadership; the product is building a great team. Great teams always finish well.

Great leaders never insist on conformity and cookie-cutter team members. Instead, they prefer creative thinkers, competent performers and above all, team players.

Seven ways to get the best from your team

1. Create a work environment of excellence and worthy of your team members' giving a third or more of every day to it.
2. Be generous with opportunities promoting the well-being of your team. Healthy and emotionally mature people are always more productive.
3. Make sure your team is adequately prepared for the challenging opportunities you provide as their leader. Everyone wants to feel valuable and more productive.
4. Match the person to opportunity. Know their strengths and weaknesses and set reasonable expectations. Give in occasionally, it can have a powerful effect—especially in high-stress situations.
5. Give constant feedback. Never compromise the truth but find a way to share negative news in a positive

way. Remember, no one ever overdoses on encouragement.

6. Develop relational equity. Have human relationships as well as professional relationships. The relational equity you have invested must support the demand you make or the relationship weakens, first emotional then functionally.

7. Reward individual accomplishment only if it makes the team better. Superstars eventually burn out without a supportive team that causes them to shine.

Day 62
Goals—Servants or Masters?

On April 15, 1912, news of the Titanic's sinking on her maiden voyage shocked the world. 1500 of the 2200 on board lost their lives. Either people around the world blamed the ship's builders for shoddy design and construction or the ship's captain, Edward Smith for running her at full speed through a shipping lane filled with icebergs.

What many did not know is that the ship's owners, the White Star Line, sent their own representative a naval architect, Thomas Andrews, to see if the Titanic could break the speed record for crossing the Atlantic. Against the urgent advice of Captain Smith, Mr. Andrews drove the ship far beyond her reasonable limits attempting to reach the goal.

Great leaders set ambitious goals but never demand on reaching them at any cost. Goals must be achievable and sometimes stretch the team beyond what they feel is reasonable. Great leaders know where that critical point is and never go beyond it.

The benefits of reaching a goal must never outweigh the value of its achievement, especially at the cost of ruined relationships and emotional scars that may last a lifetime. Leaders are inspirational, while bosses drive their workers, most of the time for their own selfish reasons. Goals are servants, meant to inspire teams to accomplish great things, never masters to drive teams to their breaking point.

Day 63
Define Your Expectations—or Expect Disappointment

Great leaders always define the expectations with any assignment. Unfulfilled expectations bring life's greatest disappointments. Your ability to attract and retain valuable people increases in direct proportion to your ability by defining everyone's expectations from the beginning.

Good people who cannot find fulfillment and value associating with you and your team should not stay around too long. If they do, they damage the team and diminish your leadership influence in the eyes of the team.

Refresh them, retrain them or remove them—sooner rather than later!

Day 64
What Happens When Organizations Don't Think?

When it comes to developing leaders, the most common mistake organizations make is not *"thinking it through."* Great organizations take the time and spare no effort or expense in making sure leadership development is well planned and executed.

Organizations that get involved in leadership development without doing the necessary hard thinking exhibit the following symptoms:

1. There is no clear concept of what strategic leadership is and how it relates and functions with daily management activities.

2. There is little understanding of the different levels of leadership, and the priorities, training, and execution strategy peculiar to each level.

3. Commitment, and many times, even a casual interest for leadership development is lacking at all levels.

4. Leadership education and training efforts often reflect the latest fads—not the components critical for success.

5. Everyone is looking for the quick fix, instant quality leadership, and when it's not forthcoming, everyone looks for another silver bullet.

6. They seldom ask the right questions and demonstrate the patience to consider all possible solutions, *"ready—fire—aim"* is the common strategy.

7. They are vulnerable to the *"experts"* selling leadership solutions at a price rarely matching their practical value.

The second most common error non-thinking organizations make is the unconscious assumption that leadership development starts and stops with the senior leaders.

In most organizations, the lion's share of available resources for leadership development is invested in the top leadership and management positions. Only the leftovers, usually very little, is invested in the front-line team members—those having the most contact with customers and members and doing the lion's share of the work.

Day 65
All you Need to know About Selecting Future Leaders

"Measure the cloth seven times because it can only be cut once" —Russian Proverb.

How do you know if people have the potential to lead effectively or are they better suited to support those already leading?

There are four possible routes to leadership: *Emergent*—someone emerges in a *"leaderless group"* situation, perceived as the right person to lead, and elected by informal acclamation, examples, Gandhi, Lawrence of Arabia, and Martin Luther King. By *appointment*—assigned by a superior to whom they remain accountable. *Elected*--the group establishes the right to choose their own leader and the leader remains accountable to the electors. Through *heredity*—leadership influence obtained by birth and relationship, called nepotism.

Seven questions you should ask when considering future leaders

1. Are they team builders or silo builders?
2. Are there any issues about their integrity, enthusiasm, commitment, honesty, fairness, confidence, or their ability to make the tough decisions?
3. If task focused, do they still find time for teambuilding and individual development?

4. Relative to the group they will be leading, do they have the professional skills/technical ability that command respect?

5. Do they have the relevant experience to qualify them to lead at this level?

6. Do they exemplify the qualities required and admired by those they will lead?

7. Do they know exactly what their leadership influence is expected to produce?

Given affirmative answers to the previous questions, your future leaders should possess the following five competencies

1. Leadership and teamwork qualities: including energy, enthusiasm, initiative, and innovation.

2. Decision making and thinking skills in the applied forms of problem solving, goal setting, and creating a clear path to the future.

3. Communication skills: listening, speaking, writing, reading, and conducting effective and efficient meetings.

4. Competent in current communication and management technology.

5. Self-management: the ability to organize, manage, and lead their own life and workplace responsibilities, living a lifestyle of commitment to both.

"Nobody doubted his capacity to rule until he became emperor of Rome" Tacitus—writing about Galba.

History does seem to repeat itself at so many levels and situations. Will we ever learn, be slow to appoint to avoid having to disappoint? It is better to disappoint one person at the start rather than the whole team later on.

Day 66
Pay Attention to Your Goals—or No One Pays Attention

Before he was a famous colonel he was a sixth-grade dropout, a farm hand, an army mule-tender, a locomotive fireman, an aspiring lawyer, a ferry boat entrepreneur, a tire salesman, an amateur obstetrician, a gas station operator, a motel operator and finally, a restaurateur.

At age 65, the new I-75 highway diverted traffic away from his Corbin, KY restaurant and Colonel Sanders was left with nothing but a Social Security check and a secret recipe for fried chicken.

In 1955, confident of the quality of his fried chicken, the Colonel devoted himself to developing his chicken franchising business. Less than 10 years later, Sanders had more than 600 KFC franchises, and in 1964, he sold his interests in the U.S. Company for $2 million.

Not bad for a man who started from scratch at retirement age!

Colonel Harland Sanders is a great American success story because in spite of what most people would see as great difficulties and overwhelming odds, the Colonel saw them as great opportunities. He set new goals and refused to be defeated. The 600 franchises in less than 10 years proved not only his ability to set goals, but also his ability to get others to pay attention and his goals became *"our"* goals.

Great leaders pay more attention to their goals than to seemingly impossible challenges, negative vision drainers, or the odds for success. Poor leaders are conditioned for failure by allowing negative thinking and speaking people, regardless of how talented, to join their team. Negative people never pay attention to ambitious goals—only problems and difficulties.

Here are 7 things that will help you set *"attention getting"* goals and build a team with a winning attitude:

1. Set multiple goals that lead to living a balanced life - have some fun!
2. Set challenging goals that stretch you without discouraging you or your team.
3. Work on your goals every day, not annually, quarterly, or weekly.
4. Make a commitment--put some pressure on yourself before others start pressuring you with their goals and dreams.
5. Be careful with whom you share your dreams and goals. Hang out with balcony people and avoid basement people.
6. Remember; your words define your future, your priorities determine your goals, and your goals determine your daily action plan.
7. Write your goals out accompanied by set deadlines and highlight who is going to do what by when— otherwise you just have good ideas with no corresponding action.

"All I have is this little bitty frying pan." —Colonel Sanders, Founder KFC

Day 67
Never Overestimate Your Personal Value or Leadership Shelf Life

Leaders who refer to *"My"* business, organization, or church as a personal possession usually have an ego that cannot be confined in a football stadium. Any successful effort is built through the collective effort of many dedicated team members--Leadership 101.

Ego vs. humility is a critical balancing act. Without an ego very little of significant value happens. However, an inflated or out-of-bounds ego leaves a lot of blood on the trail in the drive to success.

According to Yale University's management psychologist Dr. Clayton Alderfer, *"Genuine leaders rarely radiate I-am-the-greatest tone."* The great leaders have a healthy mix of confidence and humility.

Naive leaders who think they're indispensable, even for a day a week much less an extended vacation, hardly understand their place in the grand scheme of life and are totally out of touch about understanding the shelf life of their leadership effectiveness.

Many myopic leaders are manipulated or dethroned by money, flattery, selfish glory, or *"they can't do it without me"* syndrome.

Although many leaders are victims of their own runaway egos, you must guard against an equally dangerous pitfall - excessive modesty or false humility. Excessive modesty is usually a sincere but a misguided self-depreciation of the value God placed in everyone He gave life. False humility is an attempt to deceive others by projecting someone you are not. Neither serves leaders well.

The Apostle Paul in Romans 12:3 said, *"Don't think more of yourself than you ought."* When you look in the mirror, list your personal abilities and accomplishments be brutally honest but not to the point of personal injury.

God only made one of you, celebrate *WHO* you are, not just what you do. Others will celebrate what you do but seldom celebrate who *YOU* are. Learn to cheer for yourself occasionally just don't inflate your value or extend your leadership shelf life beyond its expiration date.

Day 68
Great Leaders' Checklist for Creating Teamwork Excellence

1. I involve my team in planning the future and setting annual goals.
2. I explain how our action plan supports the overall effort - marketplace or church.
3. I explain what happens if we fail to successfully execute.
4. I explain the benefits if we successfully execute the plan.
5. I take time to teach, train and coach any new skills necessary for success.
6. I explain the attitude and behavioral expectations I have for individual members and the team.
7. I develop a performance agreement for all team members so there is no question about their assignment.
8. I identify experienced and gifted individuals and position them in key areas of influence.
9. I identify the "vision-drainers" and help them overcome their negatives or release them from the team.
10. We do not move forward with our strategy until the team has completed the first nine steps.

Based on a score

(1) being seldom, (3) being sometimes and (5) being often

[10-15]—Your drowning, move over let someone else lead.
[20-30]—You're in the middle of the pack, find a good coach.
[35-49]—Your in Leaderships' top twenty percent, find a young leader to coach.
[50]—No one is perfect, you need to resign, you are kidding yourself!

What changes do you need to make, how do you plan to make them, and how are you going to implement them?

Day 69
Great Leaders Consistently Ask Questions

1. Do all team members have the skills to competently serve our organization and win in their assigned task? What adjustments do you need to make?
2. How well does everyone understand and passionately support our mission, vision, values and strategy? How will we handle those who cannot or will not?
3. Do all team members place a high value on finishing, maintaining a winning attitude and vocabulary, stay on a continuous learning curve and display emotional maturity under pressure?
4. Is every team member committed to the team and a teamwork culture for delivering measurable results?

If you want to see, your vision is a reality you cannot ignore these four checkpoints. Let them be daily speed bumps and energizing points to help you and your team creates momentum and success.

Never forget, great leaders ask good questions, good leaders respond to questions and poor leaders have all the answers.

Day 70
Building a Culture of Trust

Great leaders continually build a culture of trust—the glue of every team and the lubricant of every win. A culture of trust has the following components:

1. Shared accountability—no one escapes.
2. Shared commitments—everyone shares the responsibilities and work load.
3. Open and honest communication based on accurate and adequate information—is the minimum not the goal.
4. No secrets or surprises, these are for kids parties—not a grownup work environment.
5. DWYSYWD as a way of life—"Do what you say you will do."

Where are the weak areas on your team and in your work environment—what do you plan to do about, when and how?

Day 71
Great Leaders do Three Things for Their Team

The Bible is the greatest leadership manual ever written. Corporations, organizations, and churches that are the most profitable, effective and sustainable use biblical principles whether they understand them, agree with, or promote them.

There is a story in Joshua 1:9-15 that illustrates this truth. Here are three leadership principles found in that text:

1. "Be strong and courageous" (v.9). Your leadership significance expands or shrinks in proportion to the risk. Strength and courage are not demonstrated through great speeches but through predetermined actions. You can follow from a distance but you can't lead from there.

2. "Crossover ahead of your brothers" (v.14). Leaders are always ahead of the vision because they remain passionate about the mission. They don't possess the mission—the mission possesses them. They teach their team the importance of expectation management and how to lead to the future—not just win today.

3. "Help your brothers" (v.14c). How long do you invest in your team—until they "possess the land." The race is not finished until every team member crosses the finish line. Team success should never cause personal discouragement or failure.

When leaders do what they are meant to do - the reason you are called "Leader," your team will respond as Joshua's did in Verse 16: "And they answered Joshua, 'We will do whatever you command us, and we will go wherever you send us."

Relational dividends through teamwork doesn't just happen, you have to make strategic plans and focus everyone's effort. Relational skills and a spirit of teamwork must have value above technical skill and position all the time.

Day 72
Great Leaders Don't Live in Denial

"Denial is a state of rational apprehension that does not result in an appropriate action." —Peter Gay

General Electric is the only remaining firm from the original Dow Jones Industrials established in 1896. On average 10% of all companies, disappear every year. Over 3,000 churches and organizations close annually. Denial is the major reason for this constant failure.

You cannot live in denial very long about what you can do, your skill level, everyone knows soon enough if you can perform. Too many leaders live in denial about *"who"* they are and refuse to take responsibility. Living with others is tough, but living with people who are living in denial is tougher, especially leaders.

Great leaders are easy to follow because they do not hide who they are behind their reputation and performance record. They are honest about their strengths and weaknesses. They take corrective action based on the recommendations of a good coach and allowing honest feedback from their team members without retaliating.

This *"knowing of you"* takes time, a spirit of humility, transparency, and a willingness to confront weaknesses, fears, insecurity, and blind spots. Great leaders are a joy to follow because they are first in line for this inspection before they start inspecting the troops.

Day 73
Great Leaders Excel at Critical Task

Success is difficult if you don't excel at the tasks that are critical to the organization you lead. Sounds simple but too many leaders, especially entry level, inexperienced, untrained leaders, fail to identify, and stay focused on the 3-4 most important activities that give them the best return for their time, energy and resources.

Four things all great leaders prioritize

1. Relentless focus on those 3-4 tasks critical to their success.
2. Never engage in any effort that does not have a clear strategy driven by goals.
3. Manage well the events and promises that create the demand on their leadership.
4. Continual development of the skills necessary for their success and maximize their use.

You can put out fires, unplanned interruptions that may or may not be urgent, or focus on your critical tasks. However, you cannot do them both well at the same time. Your staff is for firefighting, as a leader your job is keeping fires from starting.

Great leaders are disciplined and passionate about matching their own priorities, and those of their team, with what is critical for advancing the vision, not every blimp appearing their radar screen.

Day 74
Great Leaders Feed on Courage and Conviction

Why? Because leaders are surrounded every day with hurting, breaking or broken people. People bring a lot of "stuff" to the marketplace and church...failed relationships, financial challenges and health issues.

It takes courageous leaders to build people and not just a business, church or organization. Courage to do the following:

1. Courage to stretch beyond your comfort zone and inspire your team to do the same.
2. Courage to look in the mirror before looking out the window when assigning blame and look out the window before looking in the mirror when giving credit.
3. Courage to take personal responsibly for your decisions and actions and challenge your team to do the same.
4. Courage to live your moral and ethical convictions even if it brings temporary personal hurt.
5. Courage to build a life-changing environment for your team that has a positive impact on everyone that touches them or the service they provide.

Day 75
Great Leaders Feed on Courage and Conviction—
Part 2

Having moral opinions is not the same as having moral convictions. You will argue for your opinions but you will die for your convictions. We admire people, who have the courage to take a stand in the face of adversity and honor their convictions when convictions are biblically based they bring value to others.

Here are seven that serve most great leaders well

1. They believe in people and worth the investment to develop, empower and deploy.
2. They believe in telling the Truth - honesty, telling it all the time—integrity, even if it is uncomfortable.
3. They believe in servant-leadership leadership models and shun command and control type models.
4. They believe in the brevity of life, the uncertainty of tomorrow and living each as if it were their last.
5. They believe that great individual talent may not always be the best fit for their team.
6. They believe in being a hope dealer for tomorrow - not a dream killer.
7. They believe you must win the hearts and minds of people before you ask for hands and feet.

Courage and conviction—the breakfast of all Champions!

Day 76
Give Up Your Right and Find Greatness in Serving Others

Note the paradoxical style of Jesus' leadership: He was gentle as a lamb—yet was the Lion of Judah. He was meek—yet aggressive when cornered by injustice. He was gregarious—yet spent much of His time alone. He had no formal education—yet taught as one having authority. He was a friend to the outcast-yet dined with the elite.

Head table seats are by invitation only. Greatness is not a measurement of self-importance but self-abandonment. If the other ten disciples had understood that leadership is not about position—James and John's request would not have threatened them.

The position you hold or the greatness of the task you perform has little to do with God's call on your life. Two characteristics of servant-leaders are humility and the ability to wait. Humility is the balance to giftedness.

We have too many Burger King leaders—*"I'll have my way."*

Day 77
Balcony People vs. Basement People

Great leaders hang out with balcony people and avoid basement dwellers. Balcony people have an elevated view of life and calling. They look over a lot of stuff, can see a long way, know where they are going, and why.

Basement people cannot see very far, the view is cluttered and their vision is limited. Therefore, whether you lead in the marketplace or the church, both have basement people you must avoid. They are called vision drainers.

Kingdom leadership is relationship driven. Develop relationships with people who celebrate you and your vision— not just tolerate you and your dream. You will always find them in the balcony.

Day 78
Great Leaders Have 7 Strong Team-Building Skills

1. They create a shared vision for today's opportunities and tomorrow's possibilities.
2. They build a highly energized and cooperative team around a compelling mission, credible values and a realistic strategy.
3. They build effective partnerships within their own organization and other organizations globally.
4. They share their leadership influence and victories without feeling threatened.
5. They recruit, teach, train, and deploy, quality team players, team leaders and leaders of leaders.
6. They put teamwork and team accomplishments above individual efforts no matter how great they are--no superstars on their team.
7. They make everyone accountable—including the one they look at in the mirror every day.

Do not be so busy managing the task, building your reputation and resume that you fail in developing your team-building skills. The "big money" always goes to those who can build teams or sell the Brooklyn Bridge.

Day 79
Partners or Opponents?

Great leaders find a way for everyone to win as long as— everyone stays in the game with a sincere desire to create a win for everyone, not settle for a compromise, or take their *"marbles"* and go home.

Comprise is a tool for managers and politicians, but a very weak leadership style. When you use the win-win approach to conflict, you change the culture of adversity and defense to one of a cooperative spirit and a collaborative effort.

One person consistently applying a joint problem-solving approach can make a significant difference to any conflict. If you are a core leader, you must be that person. You must convince yourself that redirecting the course and tone of the conflict is worth the effort, if not, do not expect it from the team.

Until you pay attention, you are usually unaware of the way you argue your own ideas. You often find yourself with a knee-jerk reaction in difficult situations, based on your long established habits combined with the mood of the moment.

When challenged, only the mature do not separate and disconnect from those causing them pain and difficulty. Too many times it becomes a *"you against me"* and a sense that I must win at any cost. With the spiritual giants, it is always, "I've heard from God."

I get nervous around two kinds of Christians; those who never hear from God, and those who are always hearing from God but never anyone else. Most conflicts are not about hearing from God but listening with your heart and not just your head to each other.

Often it is no longer, what is best for everyone but my way is the only solution. The most important decision at this point is changing the conversation from looking at solutions back to what are the underlying needs of all parties.

Addressing each person's needs rather than a single solution, means building a solution that acknowledges and values those needs, not denying others' and justifying your own.

Great leaders ask questions like, *"Why does that seem like the best solution to you?" "What's your real need here?" "What are the team's best interests in this situation?" "What values are important to you here?" "What's the outcome you want to see?"*

The answers to these questions significantly alter the conversation and determine at the end of the day if you have a partner or an opponent!

Day 80
Playing Out of Position

In 1993 at the peak of his career, three-time NBA finals MVP Michael Jordon left the Chicago Bulls and joined the Birmingham Barons, a minor league baseball team. As a basketball player, he dominated but as a baseball player, he is barely a footnote. Why, he gave the same the same effort and dedication to both sports, but in one he excelled and the other he failed. What made the difference?

Michael Jordon is a classic example of how an enormously talented person can fail when he out of position. Jordon was a world-class basketball player because that sport matched bests his physical attributes, desire and experience. He grew up playing against older players and received excellent coaching at all three developmental levels high school, college and the pros.

A 2012 Gallup study indicated that only 50% of all U.S. workers maximize their strengths everyday on the job, probably less in the nonprofit sector. It further showed that hundreds of thousands of others would be more effective if placed in another position in the same company.

Maximizing the gifts, talents and strengths of your team begins with understanding *"who"* they are, not looking at their resume that describes their educational preparation, work experience, and cherry-picked endorsements. Who a person is, is the person within the package. Their performance is coming out of that package. Don't wait for Christmas to open the package and find they are playing out of position.

Playing people in the right position increases their energy, team morale, task engagement, and productivity while reducing their frustration and reducing staff turnover—a goal of every leader. Many times, solving your performance expectations is directly related to getting the right person in the position.

After 47 years of building teams and developing leaders, in both profit and nonprofit organizations, I can guarantee you there are no ideal team members but there is an ideal position that every team member plays their best game, and it is your job as their leader to help them find it. Playing people out of position never gets better with age, make the changes sooner rather than later—everyone is happier!

Day 81
Help People Switch Frames

Great leaders help their team members learn how to switch or adjust their frame—their way of thinking and gain a new perspective. How you frame an issue creates your perception of the challenge and how you go about solving it.

1. Problem Frame—you see everything as a problem.
2. Learning Frame—you see everything as a learning opportunity.
3. Detail Frame—microscopic view, you focus on one issue.
4. Big Picture Frame—telescopic—you focus overall.
5. Personal Frame--you focus on what is happening to me.
6. Team Frame—you focus on what is affecting the team.
7. Conflict Frame—you focus on conflicts.
8. Reconciliation Frame--you focus on resolving issues.

Teach your team to switch frames

1. Problem Frame to Learning Frame. *"What are some options for us?"*
2. Personal Frame to Team Frame. *"What is best for the team?"*
3. Detail Frame to Big Picture Frame. "Can we step back for a moment from the microscope?"

4. Conflict Frame to Reconciliation Frame. *"What do think would motivate them to consider something else?"*

Only a fool puts a death-grip on a certain way of thinking when it is obvious it's no longer working. Much of your success as a leader is determined by how well you help people gain a new perspective while staying energized by the vision and remaining a team player.

Day 82
Influence Their Thinking—Not Control Their Behavior

Great leaders influence thinking instead of trying to control behavior. They learn why team members perform as they do in critical situations.

Performance improves in direct proportion to your ability to influence their thinking. Poor performance is a product of poor thinking and attitude.

Great leaders influence two questions team members think about constantly. Can I succeed and is there any value for me? How they answer these two questions determines their performance.

Do not assume you know the answer. If you do not influence their thinking, you can be sure others will. If you are not happy with someone's performance find out what he or she are thinking. If you have earned their respect, they will tell you the truth.

Day 83
What Stops You?

"Before success comes in any man's life, he's sure to meet with much temporary defeat and, perhaps some failures. When defeat overtakes a man, the easiest and most logical thing to do is quit. That's exactly what the majority of men do."—Napoleon Hill

Nothing can stop you—if

1. You have identified your governing values. You will argue for your convictions—but you will die for your values. What three to five core values govern your life? If you hesitate or just do not know, then you are a product of someone else's values. There are many valuable things you could do with your life; but great leaders are passionate about the one that rises above all others. What's yours? If you do not know, you can be stopped.

2. You have set goals that help you do something about those values. A goal is planned conflict with the status quo. To pursue a goal, you must do something new, leave the familiar, get out of your comfort zone, and explore new frontiers.

3. You are determined, a made up mind is a battle won. You persevere until you win. Be like a stamp, stick to it until arriving at the pre-determined destination without a return address. Memorize Ella Wheeler's poem,

Will

"There is no chance, no destiny, no fate, that can circumvent or hinder or control that firm resolve of a determined soul."

Jesus said, *"Nothing shall be impossible unto you."*
—Matthew 17:20

"Success is going from failure to failure without losing enthusiasm."—Winston Churchill

The reason most people never achieve their dreams is because they simply quit—give up too soon. Life was never meant to be easy. Without struggle, nothing develops whether it is a butterfly, acorns, or you. Remember, the times where it is most important to persevere are the times that you will be most tested.

"Effort only fully releases its reward often you refuse to quit."—Napoleon Hill

Day 84
Why Not Your Best?

A few years ago on the TV program, Jeopardy, the final question was *"How many steps does the guard take during his walk across the Tomb of the Unknown Soldier?"* All three contestants missed it. The correct answer is 21, alluding to the 21-gun salute, the highest honor given any military or foreign dignitary.

Those who guard the memorial to the unknown fallen heroes make the following commitments:

* Live 2 years in a barracks beneath the tomb.
* Cannot drink alcohol on or off duty for the rest of their lives.
* Cannot swear in public for the rest of their lives.
* Cannot disgrace the uniform in any way.

After their two years is up they are given a wreath to wear signifying they served at the tomb, presently less than 700 are worn today. The guards must obey these rules for the rest of their lives or surrender the wreath.

Webster describes *BEST* as being *"the most excellent, surpassing all others in the most excellent manner in the most suitable way."* The word best occurs 25 times in scripture from Genesis 43 to 1 Corinthians 13. In Genesis 44, Pharaoh told Joseph to give his family the best land in Egypt, the father in Luke 15 told his servants to give his prodigal son the best robe, and the Apostle Paul in 1 Corinthians 13 said, *"Covet earnestly the best gifts."*

Great leaders, regardless of the opportunity, give their very best in three ways:

First, they give their best energies to their most important relationships their God, their family (natural and spiritual), and their marketplace ministry.

Second, they give their best resources to their highest priorities; their *"seed"* their tithes and offerings to expand God's Kingdom on earth, their savings for investment in their family's future, and stewarding all other resources wisely in living life to its fullest.

Third, they give their best attitudes to their deepest disappointments. They develop a *Spirit of Love* for those who would harm them, a *Spirit of Faith* for unanswered prayer, and a *Spirit of Hope* for the best days that are yet to come.

God gave you his very best in his only Son - Jesus. Jesus gave us his very best from making furniture in his dad's carpenter shop to dying on the cross in our place.

If you aren't giving your very best to every task, every day—why not?

Day 85
Great Leaders Earn Respect—Not Demand it

You can demand obedience from those on your team but only from those who are fearful or lack confidence. However, the fearful or those lacking confidence will let you down at critical times when you need them the most.

Sometimes even those who respect you and your leadership are not always the easiest to lead but you can count on them when the chips are down and tough decisions have to be made. How do you earn that respect?

1. Get to know your followers by constantly building relational equity. You can never have too many deposits in their emotional bank accounts.
2. Gaining respect involves being competent in what your leadership position demands and keeping your word.
3. Create a zone of separation where your followers cannot come. In that zone, you create things for them they cannot provide for themselves. Without that zone, familiarity sets in and respect fades.
4. Respect for your leadership begins and develops on the front lines where your team members live, not watching power points and listening to pep talks in meetings you control.
5. Future leaders learn respect by watching *"adults"*--not people in positions of power or authority displaying childish behavior.

Without respect, you may be their boss but you will

never be their leader. Respect and compliance are both given, which does your leadership deserve?

Day 86
All You Need to Know About Selecting Future Leaders

"Measure the cloth seven times because it can only be cut once" —Russian Proverb.

How do you know if people have the potential to lead effectively or are they better suited to support those already leading?

There are four possible routes to leadership: *Emergent*—someone emerges in a *"leaderless group"* situation, perceived as the right person to lead, and elected by informal acclamation, examples, Gandhi, Lawrence of Arabia, and Martin Luther King. By *appointment*—assigned by a superior to whom they remain accountable. *Elected*—the group establishes the right to choose their own leader and the leader remains accountable to the electors. Through *heredity*—leadership influence obtained by birth and relationship, called nepotism.

Seven questions you should ask when considering future leaders:

1. Are they team builders or silo builders?
2. Are there any issues about their integrity, enthusiasm, commitment, honesty, fairness, confidence, or their ability to make the tough decisions?
3. If task focused, do they still find time for teambuilding and individual development?
4. Relative to the group they will be leading, do they have the professional skills/technical ability that command respect?

5. Do they have the relevant experience to qualify them to lead at this level?
6. Do they exemplify the qualities required and admired by those they will lead?
7. Do they know exactly what their leadership influence is expected to produce?

Given affirmative answers to the previous questions, your future leaders should possess the following five competencies

1. Leadership and teamwork qualities: including energy, enthusiasm, initiative, and innovation.
2. Decision making and thinking skills in the applied forms of problem solving, goal setting, and creating a clear path to the future.
3. Communication skills: listening, speaking, writing, reading, and conducting effective and efficient meetings.
4. Competent in current communication and management technology.
5. Self-management: the ability to organize, manage, and lead their own life and workplace responsibilities, living a lifestyle of commitment to both.

"Nobody doubted his capacity to rule until he became emperor of Rome" —Tacitus—writing about Galba.

History does seem to repeat itself at so many levels and situations. Will we ever learn, be slow to appoint to avoid having to disappoint? It is better to disappoint one person at the start rather than the whole team later on.

Day 87
Vision—Your Dream for the Future

Great leaders know how vision lifts and inspires. It is what sustains everyone during times of conflict or discouragement in the pursuit of ambitious goals.

It is not just in the future, an ideal to obtain someday, somewhere, somehow. Too many leaders say, *"I'll have it someday; one day I'll finish, someday it's going to work."*

Great organizations, companies and ministries live their vision every day. It is a force, a spirit of faith that exists in the present and affects everything and every person on the team.

Your vision must be an ideal present reality that attracts people, makes them better and inspires them to follow your leadership to victory. It worked for the greatest visionary of all time—Jesus of Nazareth and it will work for you.

Day 88
Great Leaders Lead Themselves Before Leading Others

Great leaders lead themselves well before they try to lead others. Jesus, the greatest leader whoever walked the earth, knew who He was and why He came. He did not look back from the cross and say, *"Wow, I must be the Son of God."* He regularly visualized the success of His life and the life of everyone He met.

You will never be a great leader until you master yourself before you lead anyone else. You will never master yourself until you master your tongue. Your words define your future. Jesus was always speaking powerful, loving and confident words about himself because He knew whom His father was.

You never build people and lead them to victory by diminishing who you are in Christ.

There is a fine line between arrogance and confidence. Make sure you stay on the right side of the line if you want to be a great leader.

Day 89
Great Leaders Keep Things Simple

Great leaders make things simple while managers make things complex. When Jesus arrived on the scene, the religious managers had increased the rulebook to at least 365 commandments.

Being the greatest leader of all time He said, *"Let's make things simple, there are just two commandments and if you keep them you will fulfill all the others."* If you are a leader, you should be looking for ways to simplify and make things easier for your team members in this very complex world.

Never forget, leading an organization is far different than managing it.

Day 90
Great Leaders Personal Checklist

1. Others and especially those I lead on a daily basis recognize my leadership skills.

2. I regularly identify my strengths and weaknesses and look for outside help to nurture my strengths and neutralize my weaknesses.

3. My leadership development efforts include a written improvement plan addressing specific issues and legitimate goals.

4. My leadership character is evidenced by a clear set of values and leadership philosophy that I model consistently.

5. My commitment to developing my team members includes hiring, mentoring, and coaching high potential leaders who "lead" regardless of position or title.

6. My capacity to inspire others is evidenced by an atmosphere of collaboration with highly energized team members.

7. My capacity for perspective and leadership wisdom is broad and deep and I can observe and participate in the process.

8. During times of stress or conflict, I am generally aware of my own feelings, sense feelings of my team members, and actively support others in reducing tension in productive ways.

9. My ability to lead teams toward discipline, execution, and accountability is a major strength

and my team consistently delivers high quality results on time and on budget.

10. I make a consistent effort to achieve and maintain a healthy lifestyle balance including diet, exercise, time alone, time with family and most of all time to renew my spirit with God my creator.

Day 91
Who Do You Trust?

When I grew up in the 50's *"To Tell The Truth"* was a very popular TV program. It featured four celebrities attempting to correctly identify a described contestant with an unusual occupation. Two impostors who pretend to be the central character accompany this central character. The impostors are allowed to lie but the central character is sworn, *"To tell the truth."*

In the past nine years, traveling 250+ days per year, I've talked with several thousand leaders at all levels. Trust is a major issue in almost every conversation. Most people do not feel their leader is an imposter but feel their leader struggles with communicating in a style and at a level they understand.

Great leaders don't invest heavily in marketing their product or services to the public without investing substantially in their internal customers (core team) building trust. They do not make the fatal assumption by assuming their key leaders know everything they need to know. You can give too much information but you can never over-communicate.

The experienced and emotionally mature leader knows that the *"grapevine"* is more powerful than any official channel but don't use it as an excuse for poor or inadequate communication—the number one trust building tool of all great leaders.

When trust is present you cannot contain it, it overflows to every part of the organization. Without it, you have to have more corporate police officers operating the grapevine. Leaders who want to build more trust and sustain it must be visible to the stakeholders, available, and accountable to their core leaders.

Absentee leaders or leaders insulated by an assistant who also functions part-time as a Prussian guard erodes team spirit and with it, mutual trust.

Building trust most often requires sharing inside information and including core leaders in decision-making, especially the significant decisions affecting their personal future. Caution, trusting unproven or inexperienced people can be tantamount to pinning a *"kick me"* sign on your back. On the other hand, not trusting your proven core leaders diminishes their trust in you and their passion for the mission.

Breaking trust should be addressed immediately and a clear path to restoration established sooner rather than later. These things never get better with age. Trust broken the second time should bring an immediate release.

The best way to confirm and affirm those whom you trust is their ability to keep a confidence. The best time to assess their trustworthiness is before a situation arises for the need...*"to tell the truth."* Never risk your leadership with people you do not trust or with people who do not trust you.

Day 92
Leaders Provide Light for the Future—Managers Provide Directions

Great leaders are laser beams providing the power to cut through any obstacle because they focus all their energy on one single point at any given moment. Good leaders are flashlights--provide enough light for the team to accomplish today's task but little to light the path forward. Poor leaders are strobe lights--inconsistent at best or blinding at worst. The word strobe has a Greek origin, *"strobos,"* meaning the *"act of whirling"* you never know which direction they're going to shine next.

Which light describes your leadership and the energy of your team? The success of your organization is directly related to the amount of energy your people are willing to invest and your ability as its leader to harness and focus that energy toward a single burning purpose.

You as a leader can profit immeasurably through utilizing the following

1. The concentration of your people's energy focused on organizational change—improving today and planning a compelling future.
2. The power of choice as a strategy and not just an option to inspire commitment for change. Poor leaders hand their team a plan and their only choice is saying yes or no.
3. Collaborating with your team by engaging their natural desire to improve their daily efforts and create a compelling future. Change is something you do with

your team--not for or to them.

This change process involves three sequential steps

1. **ENVISION**—develop a well-lighted and articulated picture of today's task, the path forward, and how they relate.
2. **PREPARE**—find the shortest and most effective path between today and your final destination.
3. **DELIVER**—execute the change process, the blueprint for your vision. Every day you delay reduces the shelf life of your ability to lead with effectiveness.

Too many leaders have less than a compelling vision, a poorly planned action plan, or the wrong light trying to find the path forward.

Psalm 119:105 says, *"Your word is a lamp to walk by and a light to illumine my path."* Christian marketplace leaders have no excuse for leading with anything less than the strongest light beam available. They should be leading the way when others are stumbling around in the dark.

Day 93
Great Leaders Recognize and Leverage Knowledge Ability and Passion

Most people have latent talents, abilities, and existing skills that the average leader fails to recognize much less exploit. Why, because they focus too much on finishing the task at the cost of developing the individuals doing the task. Turning those talents from potential to capability is what great leadership is all about.

Recognizing and leveraging capabilities is leadership's number one priority and critical for long-term success. Let your managers focus on the numbers and task completion goals. Numerous studies over the past 50 years confirm that people by nature have four strong emotional needs connected to great performance:

- Engage in interesting and productive activities
- Succeed at new challenges
- Improve their competence for their assignments
- Demonstrate mastery over their emotional maturity

Why do so many team members feel disengaged at the prospect of job-related growth and development? In addition, why does the average leader believe that developing underperforming team members is too much effort for too little return?

Great leaders understand that repairing this disconnect requires rethinking how you develop individuals while building a team. They help everyone think like a leader—not just a team member doing his or her job.

To leverage potential you first have to recognize it. You must match individual potential to their emotional needs if you them to demonstrate competence and the desire to for team success, not just a desire for personal success.

Great leaders always see more in their team members than the team members see personally. They always believe the team can accomplish more than the team believes is possible. Great leaders are gifted in recognizing talent, creating team synergy, and leveraging both to accomplish what others only dream of—that is why they lead and not follow.

Day 94
Great Leaders Resist Recognizing Only Top Performers

All great organizations are built on a lot of good middle producers and a few outstanding performers who have learned to deal with their ego in a healthy way.

Every team member not only deserves recognition, but also requires it—both individually and for team results. Most people scramble for it and feel starved without it.

Recognition and respect is the energy that fuels the human spirit. Great leaders fuel all team members--not just the top performers. Don't wait till their on empty, top off their tanks every day!

Great leaders use healthy relationships to inspire people while poor leaders bully people using fear and manipulation. Manipulation is using fear or misguided incentives for producing short-term gains without concern for the long-term problems it creates.

Productive individuals and teamwork is the result of great leaders instilling confidence and recognizing their good middle producers while allowing them to share in the limelight created by the team's superstars. Great teams have both!

Day 95
Great Leaders Solve the Impossible

"The man who keeps busy helping the man below him won't have time to envy the man above him."—The Henrietta Mears Story."

The current generation knows little about this great leader of the mid-20th Century.

When Dr. Mears came to the First Presbyterian Church of Hollywood in 1928, there were 400 in Sunday School. When she left, there were 4,000. Such notables as Bill Bright, Billy Graham and Richard Halverson were among her students. Disappointed by the lack of sound Christian education materials she started her own publishing company in her garage that became Gospel Light Publications.

Motivated by the lack of a good Christian retreat facility for the overcrowded Los Angeles area she purchased a $350,000 facility for $30,000 known as Forest Home. It is still one of the top retreat centers in America located in the beautiful San Gabriel Mountains.

Poor leaders run away from or deny tough problems exist. Good leaders define the problem but many times just learn to live with it. Great leaders refuse to accept anything but total victory. They do not stop until they have a built a team that solves the "impossible." What you tolerate you will never change.

The Bible says in Luke 1:37, *"For with God nothing is impossible."* The capacity of your leadership is determined by what it takes to stop you! Great leadership is about solving the impossible - not managing someone else's solutions. God chose the challenges you face today especially for you, because He put within you the ability to solve them. The willingness and determination part is your responsibility.

Day 96
A Quick Guide for Orchard Growers

How soon organizations forget, there is no such thing as instant/effective leadership. Leadership development is a lot like growing fruit trees—others will probably benefit from the trees you plant. Great trees start with good seeds or stock. When picking potential leaders, pick people with the personal leadership basics already in place integrity, trustworthiness, passion for success and significance and guided by a servant's heart.

Choose people that have leadership gifting and potential. Great care and attention given to poor seed still produces mediocre trees. Plant more trees than you need because, for whatever reason, some seedlings never make it to excellence, otherwise you fill leadership opportunities with inferior leaders regardless how personable and committed the individual.

Seven step guide for leadership orchard growers

1. *Prepare the soil:* Check your organization's culture, does it grow or stunt leadership growth? You may need to plough up yesterday's model and mindset about leadership and management.
2. *Enrich the soil:* Fertilize, water, and make sure the sun has access to integrity, justice, and fairness. Remove the jungle foliage and weeds that obscure the path to these and other core values.
3. *Rotate the crops:* Give your leaders a variety of challenges and opportunities, do not burn them out

but neither bore them, both cause great people to leave you.

4. ***Let the fields lay fallow:*** Not all trees bear fruit every year, even the most productive trees need times of rest. Give your leaders time to think, reflect, and catch up.

5. ***Observe where plants thrive:*** A leader who struggles in one field may thrive in another.

6. **Prune the dead wood:** Be slow to plant (assign positions) but quick to prune (trim non-productive limbs), pluck up (replant) and burn (release to another farmer) if necessary. Abandon anything that is no longer effective, consistently return to the basics.

7. **Let the tap roots go deep:** The water of support and inspiration lie deep underground. Trees that grow and flourish year after year have deep roots.

Every organization needs one person responsible for growing, educating and training future and present leaders. The content, process, and execution must be relevant, timely and productive. Most of all, the training must enhance the mission, vision, values and strategy.

Day 97
Managing Today or Creating Tomorrow

"All men dream: but not equally. Those who dream by night in the dusty recesses of their minds wake in the day to find it was vanity, but the dreamers of the day are dangerous men for they act out their dream with open eyes to make it possible."—T.E. Lawrence

There are two basic kinds of leaders, those who solve today's problems known as managers, and those who create the future know as strategic thinkers. Both are vital for success, but everything goes better when the team leader has strategic planning skills and above average team-building skills. If not, the team gets lost like a ball in high weeds of the details.

When managing-type leaders, energized by the details are in charge the organization loses momentum, stops its passionate pursuit of the vision and active inertia sets in. If you are the senior leader, strategic planning must be a core value and your primary function.

Do your core leaders focus more on today's problems or tomorrow's opportunities? Do you have an achievable action plan that aligns your team members' behaviors with your values and goals?

Leaders, who say they have a vision but no plan (strategy) to get there, not only amaze me but also alarm me because of the disappointment they create for their followers. Strategic planning (creating the future), directs the investment of resources, generates focused direction for the team, and accountability for the results.

Great leaders never give in to the pressures of present reality at the expense of creating a path to the future. If they do, they no longer have a future but simply a duplication of today in all their tomorrows.

If you cannot create the future, follow a leader who can. *"The future belongs to those who see the possibilities before they become obvious."* John Scully

Day 98
Managing Today or Creating Tomorrow—Part 2

"If you know your enemy and know yourself, you need not fear the result of a hundred battles. If you know yourself but not the enemy, for every victory gained you also suffer a defeat. If you know neither the enemy nor yourself, you will succumb in every battle."—The Art of War

You will never create a better tomorrow until you understand the challenges facing your progress, the strategic thinking process, and when to act. The purpose of strategic thinking is improving our ability to shape and adapt to unfolding circumstances so your team determines the way forward and not unanticipated events.

Strategic planning is hard work requiring objectivity and many times a painful look in the mirror. Without defining present reality with brutal honesty—you are not ready for today much less tomorrow.

Good strategic plans—properly executed include

- Clarity on your mission, vision, and values.
- Improves the decision-making process.
- Helps anticipate and productively manage change.
- Aligns everyone's priorities.
- Establishes performance expectations identifying strengths and weaknesses.
- Provides options not previously considered.
- Creates and maintains a culture of improvement.
- Brings a sense of urgency to issues critical for success.

- Eliminates non-productive behaviors.
- Challenges assumptions and the status quo.

A leading cause of organizational failure is the lack of long-range planning tools executed consistently by qualified strategic thinking leaders. You create a better today with better management solutions, but you only create a better tomorrow through a productive strategic planning process.

Put your managers in charge of today, but only trust your tomorrow's to leaders gifted to create them through strategic thinking and action.

Day 99
Giving Information is Not Communicating

Jena is a university city in Central Germany on the River Saale—population 103,000. It is the home of Zeiss, manufacturers of optical systems. In 1926, Zeiss Corporation, whose tag line is, built the world's first modern planetarium in Jena: "We make it visible." Being able to see clearly and further is a trademark of the city.

Leaders are often frustrated and express it by saying, *"They just don't get it. I've told them, and told them, and told them."* Seems like frustrated leaders do not get it; communicating is more than giving information and telling— it knows your team members understand you, your intent, and the content of your message. If you are not sure, do not blame them for lack of performance.

Effective communication is the lifeline of any successful organization. Leaders must make sure they are sending the right message, at the right time, and to the right people. They must make sure the intended message is received, understood, and creating the desired results.

Speed, transparency, and scrutiny are the currency of today's fast paced world. In turn, this has forced leaders to increase their agility to make changes quicker and more often, and make all forms of communication more effective and efficient.

Consider the following communication demands on today's leaders

- The sheer speed of modern communication globally.

- The staggering increase in the number of digital communication channel options.
- The Shifting patterns of influence through the rise of citizen and consumer demands.
- The elevated expectations of all stakeholders for a quicker response.
- Increased regulations and the consequent communication requirements.
- Aggressive pursuit of information via the internet.
- Declining levels of trust in business, especially their communications.

Key to creating leaders who communicate well is creating a framework—a framework of well understood values within which all leaders operate. The objective is insuring everyone understands what the organization expects of them not only in terms of what they need to do, but also how they should do it, and the desired results.

Does everyone on your team understand what *"doing the right thing"* really means and passionately agree? If not, you may have given the information, but you are yet to communicate. Communicating helps people see clearly and farther. Ask your front-line team members, they will tell you how clear the vision and your messages are, they stand the farthest from the source.

Day 100
Place Your Values on a Pedestal

Steuben Glass Company breaks every imperfect piece of glass no matter how small. This is a potent symbolic act but it reinforces its values in an unforgettable way. Great leaders must resolve to model their standards and values for all stakeholders—if not they should resign. The longer they hang around the more damage they do.

If you and your core leaders do not model your values, place them on pedestal, and defend them aggressively—who will? A code of values, passionately pursed, keeps an organization focused and on course when the leader is, absent and tough times come.

It is important you limit your core values to what your core team can get their hearts and minds around. Long lists are difficult to identify, model and reinforce. Everything you do should have value but not everything can be a core value.

Great leaders have differing values but common to all are integrity, accountability, diligence, perseverance, and discipline. Organizations that pursue them passionately are invariably successful regardless of their endeavor.

Core leaders, managers, and your internal customers (employees) must emphasize your values daily. Ignore them and you risk mediocrity at best, and worse, failure. Enron, Global Crossing, Tyco, Arthur Anderson and other very successful 20th Century companies, along with many churches and non-profits, self-destructed because of bankrupt value systems.

Ask most Japanese CEO's his main job and he says, *"Harmonizing values and helping his core leaders adjust to changing priorities in an ever changing marketplace environment."*

Values motivate and sustain outstanding performance and respect for the long haul. Take your values out of the desk, off the wall, ditch the brochures, and put them on a pedestal until they are a way of life. This exercise alone would transform most organizations and propel them from the middle of the pack to leading the way.

For church leaders who do not think this is important may I remind you of the values of Jesus in Matthew 5-7 and John 13-17. How about the value system of the First Century Church in Acts 2:41-47? If the Church has real marketplace influence, its foundation is a value system worth emulating and relevant where they go every day.

www.ingramcontent.com/pod-product-compliance
Lightning Source LLC
Chambersburg PA
CBHW071550200326

41519CB00021BB/6688